ADVANCED PRAISE

"A rich and delightful resource for anyone who works in the coaching space and wants to work more freely."

— David Drake, PhD, Founder and CEO at The Moment Institute, Inc.

∼

"At its heart, coaching is highly improvisational. In *Coaching with a Twist*, Betsy and Amy highlight natural links between improv and coaching practice. They explain the philosophy, context and techniques for using improvisation to improve practice."

— Dr. Robert Biswas-Diener, author of *Radical Listening*

∼

"This book is chock full of practical tips for coaches (and trainers), presented through their unique lens of humility and humanity. The Question Story game is my favorite and the lesson on Interrupting should be used in every coach training curriculum!"

— Erika Jackson, MCC, NBC-HWC, co-author of *The Coaching Psychology Manual*

"As the founder of several ICF-accredited coach training schools, I know the power of innovative learning. Having taken the *Improv for Coaches* series myself, I've experienced firsthand how this approach unlocks creativity, deepens emotional intelligence and strengthens confidence in ways traditional training often overlooks. I was so impressed that I asked Betsy and Amy to teach this work to our coach training graduates, and I'm actively integrating it into both our foundational and advanced coach training programs. This book takes what I learned from them to another level — offering even more exercises, deeper skill-building and practical applications that make it a must-have for every coach. If you're serious about elevating your coaching, this belongs on your shelf."

— Sophia Casey, MCC, Founder & CEO at ICF-accredited coach training school, ICLI RISING

"Step into the playful, transformative world of *Coaching with a Twist: Improv for Coaches*, where creativity meets mastery. Warshawsky and Salkind masterfully weave the art of improvisation with the craft of coaching, delivering a fresh, practical guide brimming with tools, exercises and facilitation insights. This book invites coaches, leaders and educators to sharpen their skills, build authentic connections and rediscover the joy of learning. Thoughtful, inspiring and fun — this is a must-read for anyone ready to embrace creativity and growth."

— Lyssa deHart, LICSW, MCC, BCC, author of *Light Up: The Science of Coaching with Metaphors*

"This is the book I've been waiting for! *Coaching with a Twist* shows what a life-giving and life-affirming process coaching can be. Betsy and Amy are the ideal companions as we find ways of bringing more fun and joy into transformative conversations."

— Prof. Christian van Nieuwerburgh, Professor of Coaching and Positive Psychology, RCSI University of Medicine and Health Sciences

COACHING WITH A TWIST: IMPROV FOR COACHES

THE DEFINITIVE GUIDE TO USING IMPROV AND PLAY TO DEEPEN COACHING AND COMMUNICATION SKILLS

BETSY SALKIND

AMY J. WARSHAWSKY

COOPER TRINITY PRESS

Copyright © 2025 by Betsy Salkind and Amy J. Warshawsky

All rights reserved. No part of this book may be used or reproduced in any manner whatsoever without prior written consent.

Published by: Cooper Trinity Press
Address all inquiries to:
Cooper Trinity Press
info@coopertrinitypress.com

Identifiers:
LCCN: 002453858
ISBN: 979-8-9986027-0-2 (paperback)
ISBN: 979-8-9986027-1-9 (E-book)

First Edition: September 2025

This book is intended for educational and informational purposes only. The authors and publisher expressly disclaim responsibility for any adverse effects, outcomes or consequences resulting from the use or application of the information presented herein.

Every attempt has been made to source properly all research material and quotes.

COOPER TRINITY
PRESS

*Dedicated to the possibilities,
which are always out there*

CONTENTS

Introduction 1

PART I
SETTING THE STAGE
1. Who This Book Is For 9
2. How to Use This Book 11
3. Rules of Improv 13

PART II
BUILDING THE STRUCTURE
4. Facilitating Improv for Coaches 19
5. Creating and Maintaining a Supportive Environment . . . 21
6. Lessons in Non-Judgment 24
7. Time Management 26
8. How to Give Feedback 28
9. Humor 33
10. Side Coaching 36
11. Co-Facilitation 38
12. Tips for Running a Group in Zoom 41
13. Running a Group in Person 46

PART III
LET'S PLAY!
Introduction to Part 3 51
Lesson Plan 1: SUCCINCTNESS 58
Lesson Plan 2: QUESTIONS 65
Lesson Plan 3: REFLECTIONS 75
Lesson Plan 4: INTERRUPTING 83
Lesson Plan 5: FOCUS AND AGENDA 92
Lesson Plan 6: INFORMATION SHARING 97
Lesson Plan 7: STAGES OF CHANGE 108
Lesson Plan 8: AMBIVALENCE 114
Lesson Plan 9: EMOTIONS 120
Lesson Plan 10: METAPHORS 126

Lesson Plan 11: SOMATICS	132
Lesson Plan 12: NEW DIRECTIONS	138
Glossary of Improv Games	145
Notes	169
Acknowledgments	173
Author Bios	177

"Creativity is not the possession of some special talent. It's about the willingness to play."

— John Cleese

"Improvisation means coming to the situation without rigid expectations or preconceptions. The key to improvisation is motion — you keep going forward, fearful or not, living from moment to moment. That's how life is."

— Bobby McFerrin

INTRODUCTION

Improvisation is the heart of coaching. It's being in the moment, listening and responding. Play and creativity are not just fun features – they're fundamental to powerful coaching.

IF YOU'RE someone who loves to grow and play — and create those opportunities for others — then understanding and experiencing the interplay of improvisation and coaching is a game-changer.

Coaching facilitates growth and change through skilled communication. It's a process in which coaches and clients connect with one another in partnership and, more importantly, the clients connect more strongly with themselves. It's about vision, possibility and moving forward. That's why leaders are being called upon to learn coaching skills to support the development of their teams and themselves.

What drew each of us to coaching was curiosity; what keeps us engaged is that it's powerful, effective and always interesting. And to our delight, we've found that the skills that come with learning to be a coach have made us better and happier people.

Ultimately, we both fell in love with coaching to the point of shifting careers. Betsy was a professional comedian and television writer, following a short stint as a Federal Reserve bank examiner. Amy was a community event producer and movement teacher with training in martial arts. Like so many coaches, we didn't leave our experience and interests behind – we brought them with us.

With a background in improv comedy, Betsy noticed that both coaching and improv embodied the same skill set; the core of each is presence and listening, and both have clear frameworks. For example, in improvisational theatre, it's important to ground a scene in space and relationship through dialogue, behavior or action. In a coaching conversation, it's imperative that the focus and agenda (aka coach-client agreement) are established and maintained.

During the five-year period in which we trained over 1,000 students in the ADAPT Health Coach Training Program, we noticed that most of them were overly serious. We wanted to help them lighten up and become more present. Their seriousness often stemmed from an inner monologue that went something like this: "Am I doing this right? What if I do it wrong? I'll never get this. I'm an idiot."

Hearing those unspoken – and sometimes spoken – words, we sought to facilitate a shift into a more resourceful state, in alignment with Barbara Fredrickson's Broaden-and-Build Theory of Positive Emotions[1] and research on Positive Emotional Attractors by Richard Boyatzis, Melvin Smith, and Ellen Van Oosten.[2] The ability to facilitate this shift is one of the things that makes coaching and improv so powerful.

For years, Betsy sought to bring her passions for improv and coaching together. One day, at the beginning of the pandemic, we were discussing how to better serve our mentor coaching clients, many of whom were at a loss because their clients' long-term goals were suddenly out the window. As we discussed the need for flexibility, Betsy said to Amy, "I've always wanted to teach an improv for coaches class." And Amy, who makes shit happen, made it happen.

As the course developed, Amy brought her expertise in somatics to create improv lessons that focus on body-based awareness and practices. This is especially important when working remotely, with its somewhat unnatural embodiment.

We started with single 90-minute sessions, soon expanded to 2 hours, and eventually heeded the requests of many students for more, creating the *Improv for Coaches*™ series. The series consists of multiple sessions (most often six) with the same group of coaches meeting regularly, forming a community of improvisers with a shared skill set. This allows for greater trust and a wider variety of improv structures to explore coaching skills and challenges. Each session has a different focus, with skills building on each other.

Four years and hundreds of students later, we realized that we had more than a course. We'd developed a methodology that quickly brings people together in a low-stakes environment for learning and connection. Using the power of (non-competitive) play, it's an approach to learning and feedback that benefits not only coaches, but also facilitators, managers, leaders, teams, parents — really all humans.

As a methodology for education, there has been extensive research about the function of play and how valuable it is in learning, growth and development.[3] In Edgar Dale's Cone of Learning,[4] active learning takes place in the realm of doing, which has a greater impact than reading, hearing, watching or listening. That is, active learning is far more useful than passive learning.

Play fosters creativity, problem-solving and social connection.[5] Plus, it's fun and good for our physical and mental health. (Unless you laugh too hard like Betsy does - sometimes giving herself acid reflux.) It can help to build confidence and lessen anxiety as it trains us to be in the moment. The more we practice improvisation, the more agile we become.[6]

The journey to coaching mastery has no end. Like our clients, we're in continuous discovery of new skills, techniques and awareness. When presented as a framework for discovery, improvisation is deeply transformational. When applied to coaching skills as a method for learning, we've found it unparalleled. Beyond this, we've been delighted to see the depth of the bonds formed within each group.

We're certainly not the first or only people making connections between improv and coaching, communication and leadership. What is unique to this book is its specific application to coaching, coach training and coaching skills.

~

WE'RE aware of the irony of writing a book about something that must be experienced; we pride ourselves on almost never having slides or giving lectures when we lead a group. "It's all in the doing," we say. But we've also had many participants ask us for a list of the exercises. And we've read books about improv that have been truly inspiring. For example, musician and author Stephen Nachmanovitch's *Free Play: Improvisation in Life and the Arts*[7] and his most recent book, *The Art of Is*.[8] His writing has given us new insight into the awesomeness of improvisation, no matter the medium.

Having said all that, the whole point of improv is that you jump in the ring. Like coaching, you can't learn improv by reading about it – you have to do it. So please use this as an instructional guide to doing – an offering of structures that you can use to experience and learn with others.

Doing the exercises in this book is an invitation to become more confident and creative, and more effective as a coach and communicator. Jump in and play. You really can't do it wrong. Get comfortable with not pre-planning or getting ahead in your conversations, and trust in the bottomless well of ideas and possibilities that we can all access at any time.

We believe the more people who use improv and coaching skills, the better our world would be. Imagine a world in which people actively listen to one another, strive to hold space with non-judgment, ask good questions and think about possibilities. And then imagine a world where people of all ages are engaged in play together, inviting each person's humor and creativity.

Have fun!
Betsy & Amy

PART I
SETTING THE STAGE

"Successful improvisation is mostly a matter of taking your thoughts out of the equation, because thinking can keep the magic from happening. You have to be open enough to let the magic happen, instead of trying to make it happen."

— Jimmy Herring

1
WHO THIS BOOK IS FOR

This book is for you if you are a coach, group facilitator, educator or any other professional (or unprofessional) person interested in coaching or communication.

Coach

There are many ways for coaches to use this book, whether you are on your own or part of a peer group. You might be a small group of coaches who get together and say, "Let's play *Last Letter* to warmup and then do some *3-Word Coaching*." Don't worry, we'll tell you how to do these later in the book. Or you may use it more formally as a self-guided course.

Group Facilitator

If you're a group facilitator looking to create more engagement and belonging, this book provides everything you need to facilitate an improv for coaches group and an impactful group experience. In addition to loads of exercises, we share our approach to facilitation and co-facilitation.

Coach Educator

If you're a coach educator, whether teaching a formal course or just looking to bring more engagement into your courses, this book provides everything you need to teach coaching skills: concepts, facilitation guidance and lesson plans.

Beyond

This book is also useful if you want to learn coaching skills to use in your personal or professional life. Betsy has even used some of the exercises for a game night with non-coaches.

Don't be intimidated by all that's in here. Start somewhere and learn through doing. This is not designed to be a book you read and put away, but a resource you can return to again and again in multiple ways.

∼

2

HOW TO USE THIS BOOK

Coach: *"I would never do that with a client."* Betsy and Amy: *"Yeah, we know. We wouldn't either - most of the time."*

IMPROV FOR COACHES is a creative approach to teaching and learning the art and practice of coaching. We believe excellence and artistry grow from joy and play. Our hope is that you use this book to make learning these skills fun and enjoyable for you and for others.

While this book has many elements of a workbook, including lesson plans for partner or group activities, there's also material about coaching, communication and facilitation skills. While much of this material is in Parts 1 and 2, each lesson plan in Part 3 contains substantive discussions of core coaching and communication skills. So, if you don't have a partner or group to play with, you can still get a lot out of all three parts.

Parts 1 and 2: Setting the Stage and Building the Structure — lay out the rules of improv, how to facilitate a group, how to give feedback — everything you need to know to most effectively use the lesson plans in Part 3.

Part 3: Let's Play — includes 12 detailed lessons that we've designed for exploring and deepening particular coaching skills.

All lesson plans include warmup exercises and improvised coaching scenarios called *Coaching with a Twist*™ as well as wisdom about the topic of that lesson. When we teach our *Improv for Coaches* classes, we often start with a non-coach-specific improv warmup followed by coach-specific warmups, leading to *Coaching with a Twist*.

But this is improv — so after you get the basic setup of the approach, feel free to mix and match or make up your own. You can certainly skip right to the exercises and games; however, for a deeper experience, we recommend reading all of Parts 1 and 2.

You'll find improv warmups (games) in two different places: in the *Lesson Plans* and in the *Glossary of Improv Games*. We've attempted to credit where we've borrowed exercises in full or in part from the world of improv. The Glossary includes the warmups that come from the improv comedy world. Sometimes we'll recommend a specific game for a particular lesson, but you can pick and choose what you like. And you might enjoy doing one or more at the start of a meeting or event.

Throughout the book, we give you options for in-person or virtual delivery. Most of you have probably attended a hybrid meeting where some people were online and others were in the room. This doesn't work for improv as it's important that everyone is on equal footing. It doesn't work great for other purposes either (e.g., funerals, birthday parties, all-hands meetings), but sometimes it's better than nothing.

∼

3

RULES OF IMPROV

"The rules of improvisation appealed to me not only as a way of creating comedy, but as a worldview. Studying improvisation literally changed my life." — Tina Fey

Rules? Why do we need rules? I thought this was supposed to be fun and games? It is. But rules are a big part of how games work. They provide an agreed-upon structure that lets us relax and play together. This is true from the simplest games like tag through the most complex multiplayer video games.

In our courses, we borrow from Tina Fey's version of the classic *Rules of Improv*. The 4 rules are:

1. **Say Yes.** Agree to step in, agree to the conversation, agree to what your partner or client is offering. Accept.

2. **Yes And.** A phrase associated with improv that's perhaps most familiar to you. "Yes And" is about accepting and then adding. In coaching we don't just listen and accept what our clients are telling us, we add — perhaps with a reflection — something we heard in our client's statement that stood out,

that they may not have noticed, or something that wasn't said out loud, a shift in energy or emotion. Coaches don't just listen empathically — they build a conversation with each client that leads to new awareness and possibilities.

3. Make Statements. Don't just ask questions. In theatrical improvisation, if we just ask our scene partner questions, we are making them do all the work. For example, if all partner A says is, "Where are we? What's happening?....." partner B has to do all the work. But if partner A instead makes statements like: "Bill, you did it again. Now we're never getting out of prison," then partner B knows he's Bill, knows where they are and knows there's history between them, and the scene builds from there. In coaching, if we only ask our clients questions, they may feel interrogated, and we're also depriving them of what we might see or notice in the conversation that may be helpful to them.

4. There Are No Mistakes. Or as we say, "There are no rules." Tina Fey shared, "There are no mistakes, only opportunities. If I start a scene as what I think is very clearly a cop riding a bicycle, but you think I am a hamster in a hamster wheel, guess what? Now I'm a hamster in a hamster wheel. I'm not going to stop everything to explain that it was really supposed to be a bike. Who knows? Maybe I'll end up being a police hamster who's been put on 'hamster wheel' duty because I'm 'too much of a loose cannon' in the field. In improv there are no mistakes, only beautiful happy accidents. And many of the world's greatest discoveries have been by accident. I mean, look at the Reese's Peanut Butter Cup, or Botox."[1]

Betsy's favorite example of a happy accident is Lasik surgery, once called radial keratotomy. It was developed in Russia after someone fell and accidentally got a shard of glass in their eye and suddenly could see with 20/20 vision. Or something like that. Amy's favorite accidental discoveries include the Slinky and Silly Putty. What's your favorite?

In setting the stage for a successful workshop or class, not only do we share the rules of improv, but we've found that additional rules are helpful on Zoom. During one class, we were playing *Made Up Yoga Poses,* in which the leader makes up a fictitious yoga pose and everyone else then does the pose. One student stood up to model her pose. Another student said, "Hang on! I have to turn my camera off for a second to put some pants on." Hence, we now have a rule that everyone must come to class wearing pants or equivalent. More of these rules and tips are shared in the next section.

PART II

BUILDING THE STRUCTURE

"Improvisation can be either a last resort or an established way of evoking creativity."

— Mary Catherine Bateson

4

FACILITATING IMPROV FOR COACHES

"We learn through experience and experiencing, and no one teaches anyone anything."
— Viola Spolin

Building the Structure encompasses what we've learned while facilitating our courses. As we improvised our way through developing the course, we figured out how to make *Improv for Coaches* work online and in person, how to manage time and how to give feedback. We've consolidated our best practices here to save you time and in some cases pain. You'll learn your own best practices by doing, though you may find this section of the book a useful resource if you run into challenges.

FACILITATING INTEGRATES a number of specific areas of skill, including creating the environment, managing time effectively and providing feedback. The level of facilitation needed depends on how big and formal your group is. You may need one or more facilitators to run a session or you may not need any, though it helps to have someone keep time.

Facilitation can be formal, like what we do in our *Improv for Coaches* courses, or it can be informal, more akin to hosting a game night. If it's a peer learning group, you may want to rotate the facilitator role.

Learning takes place in environments that invite us to relax. Play and humor are helpful in creating such environments. Facilitators can benefit the group by demonstrating lightness or even goofiness. We often do this when demonstrating an activity by deliberately offering something silly or unexpected, which allows others to do or say things when they might otherwise feel inhibited.

We typically demonstrate each *Coaching with a Twist* exercise. And as facilitators, we almost always participate in group activities. Most people feel more comfortable and less exposed if everyone in the group participates. It's very common to be nervous when first doing improv – despite the fact that we all improvise in our daily lives. So it's important to foster a supportive environment, which we'll discuss in the next section.

What if people don't want to participate?

Consent is hugely important, which is why we don't think court-ordered improv would work. So while we never force anyone to do anything, improv is not a spectator sport, so we share in advance our expectations and allow each individual to choose if improv is right for them.

5

CREATING AND MAINTAINING A SUPPORTIVE ENVIRONMENT

For improv to work, participants must feel free to take risks, explore and make mistakes. How do you create trust and safety in a short amount of time with a group of people who may or may not know one another?

Some of the methods we use to help participants come together and feel as safe as possible include:

- **Send a Preparatory Email:** Each participant receives an email prior to the start of the course. Our email reads, "For the best experience, make sure you're in a quiet, stable location (i.e., not in a moving car or an E.R.) and have a strong internet connection. You'll also want to be able to view in gallery mode so you can see all the other participants for the warm ups and group exercises, so please be on a computer or iPad (not phone). Although we love your little ones, we graciously ask that they don't come to *Improv for Coaches* to play. We go for 2 hours - so bring a drink. And finally, don't forget to wear clothes on the bottom half of your body!!"

- **Name It:** In our first session of the course, we name our intention of creating trust and safety. We acknowledge that not everyone will feel comfortable every moment of every session and we invite participants to chat with us privately if there's something they need, or to reach out to either one or both of us between sessions. If we're working with a group in person, we invite them to speak with us privately during the breaks or directly to the group. We let everyone know that we are open to feedback.

- **No Recording:** To lower the stakes and increase the feeling of comfort, we typically do not record *Improv for Coaches* sessions. We let the group know this at the beginning of our work together. Betsy tells them, "So don't worry, this won't be part of your permanent record."

- **Share the Rules:** During the first session, we share the 4 Rules of Improv. We like Tina Fey's version (see Chapter 3), as she is recognized for her skill in improv and her version is simple and to the point. If we're hosting a virtual session, we share the rules both verbally and in the chat. You do not have to share the rules of improv but we find it helpful in giving structure and it brings people into the traditions of the improv world.

- **Limit Introductions:** We want everyone in the group to quickly come into community and we don't want to use up too much time with introductions. In the first session, we ask everyone to share what they'd like to be called, where they're from, along with something more fun — "something ridiculous or surprising about you," or "a sound that expresses how you're feeling right now." Keep introductions brief to leave more time for play — a superior way to get to know each other.

- **Include Warmups:** We're thoughtful about choosing specific warmup exercises for each session. We start with one that may or may not be related to the subject of that session but is fun, easy to participate in, involves all members of the group and brings everyone into presence and connection. We usually follow that with warmups more directly related to the topic of the session. One of the warmups we often do first with a new group is the Mirror exercise (see Lesson Plan 1). In this exercise, we send participants into breakouts, usually as complete strangers. They don't come out that way.

- **Discuss Zoom Guidelines if Relevant:** We ask that all participants remain present throughout the session, minimize use of the chat feature and keep cameras on unless they check in with us individually. (More on Zoom in the next section.)

In creating and maintaining a supportive environment, you can plan for a lot, but you also need to improvise to meet emerging conditions. During the LA fires in January 2025, we had a virtual *Improv for Coaches* session scheduled. Betsy and two of our students were in LA at the time, under threat of evacuation. We decided to open the Zoom room to offer a supportive space and with the intention of rescheduling the class. After spending some time together checking in, sharing fears and tears, we asked the group about rescheduling. The students in LA requested that we stay on Zoom as long as the situation permitted and that we hold class. At the end of our time together, we all shared how much better we felt having spent the two hours in play and community.

6

LESSONS IN NON-JUDGMENT

You can't judge a book by its cover (even this one). Most of us are judging all the time whether we're aware of it or not. We all have inner monologues, some more verbose than others.

Are you kidding me?... Get out of the intersection, you jerk... Ugh, why do I always do that?... Wow, that sweater does not go with those pants... I love it... Blue is definitely not your color... They're the GOAT... Could my nose hair be any longer? ... Eww... WooHoo!... Nice suit... We have NOTHING in common... Smooth move Ex-Lax!

In coaching we are given the gift of stepping into an encounter without our judgments, which is good not only for our clients but for us. Holding our clients without judgment is an essential part of coaching. It enables us to listen to others for their intention and meaning rather than relating what they're saying to our own experiences and opinions. We have found this practice of conscious non-judgment to be one of the greatest gifts in coaching, and a gift that extends into all areas of our lives.

This opportunity to leave judgment at the door extends to facilitation. The times when we allowed judgment to sneak in, we found that we were often wrong and that our opinions rendered us less effective as mentor coaches.

> **Amy:** *I notice that when I become judgmental, it comes from a place of anxiety. I get nervous. I feel nervous for the coach. I feel nervous for the client. I feel nervous for the observers. And I feel nervous about how I'll give feedback to the coach that's both kind and effective. Noticing the judgment and the anxiety enables me to let it go and not act from it.*

Despite having to work through the discomfort of our judgments and feelings, we've been consistently surprised and delighted in witnessing creativity and growth.

Regardless of the level of experience of the participants, we can all learn and grow together. Our students who have found improvisation to be the most difficult challenged us to find better ways to design for learning — just as our most challenging clients help us grow our skills as we figure out how to be a better coach for them.

We had one student who shared that she did not like feedback – even if it was positive. This had never happened before and we were stumped about what to do. So we asked her, "What would be useful to you?" She replied, "Ask me questions."

∼

7

TIME MANAGEMENT

Managing time is a key task of the facilitator. In a coaching session, the coach is responsible for managing the time. In an *Improv for Coaches* session, the facilitator is responsible for making sure everyone gets a turn to participate and for shifting the group to the next activity as laid out in the lesson plan, unless you decide to change up the plan, which is fine.

We have seen other facilitators do an improv exercise with only a few of the participants and then have the larger group discuss it; however, we strongly recommend planning and facilitating in such a way that every person in the group gets to experience the exercise. With larger groups, this may require the use of breakouts (breaking the group into smaller groups). Improv is all about the *doing* (which is why lots of people want to perform improv, even if their friends don't always want to watch it).

> **Amy:** *When I was first mentor coaching and running group sessions for 20+ people, I would often let time run away from me. Instead of limiting the time for talking about the topic of the session, I'd let too many students ask questions, and in the end, we wouldn't have enough time for experiential learning. Through facilitating improv with Betsy, I've learned the*

value of managing time well, not only to give everyone an opportunity to learn by doing but also the importance of maintaining the agreements about how time is spent. Sometimes this means telling students to hold questions until after the exercise, as that may answer the question for them.

Betsy: *My keeping strict time to ensure that everyone gets to go comes from a value of fairness and wanting everyone to get equal time. As a stand-up comedian, there were times I was on a line-up when a show was time-limited, due to a second show, for example. If comics earlier in the line-up went over their allotted time, the comics performing later would get cut short, causing them added stress. "What, are they cutting an album? WTF? Now I have to cut out half my set!"*

In addition to managing the time carefully in the session, it's important to think about time when planning. We recently did a one-hour session but had planned too much for the hour, which didn't allow enough time for reflection and integration. After each session, we integrate our learning into the lesson plan for future use. In this case, we cut some of the activities to allow adequate time for reflection.

∾

8

HOW TO GIVE FEEDBACK

> "I'm proud of my ability to understand what somebody else is trying to do and help them achieve it, because part of the aesthetic of improvisation is service. We don't lead; we only follow. You never say no. Serve the servant, follow the follower. And that's very valuable in your life, as well as very valuable in your work."
> — Stephen Colbert

As coaches, we are dedicated to understanding what somebody else is trying to do and helping them achieve it. In *Improv for Coaches*, we are similarly dedicated.

Feedback, sometimes called feedforward, can be life-changing, both positively and negatively. We feel that it's important to be thoughtful and deliberate about how we give feedback. We've also learned the importance of how participants give feedback to one another. We never assume that people already know how to do this and always take some time to share our approach.

One way that facilitators can cultivate trust and safety in the learning environment is by guiding feedback to be supportive.

Betsy: *When I was in the Boston improv troupe* Guilty Children, *after each show the cast members would share feedback. Having been raised in a critical environment ("I tell you these things because I love you!"), I knew exactly where people had missed the mark and shared it freely with them. Dot Dwyer, a more seasoned troupe member, took me aside and taught me how we do feedback. She said that most people know what they've done wrong. They'll beat themselves up about it better than you can. But what they don't know so well is what they're doing right. And reinforcing that will make a big difference.*

This is a lesson I learn over and over again in life and coaching and is consistent with Motivational Interviewing (MI),[1] positive psychology, Appreciative Inquiry,[2] and other strengths-based approaches in coaching.

Years later, I attended Stacie Chaiken's What's the Story *writing workshop, where she shared her version of feedback. After a writer has shared, the listeners answer the following questions: What did you love? What drew you in?*

This helps the creator understand the impact on those receiving their work. Then, the listeners are asked the following: What did you want to know more about?

The recipient of the feedback is asked not to respond. Keep what's useful, discard the rest. Take anything useful into the next iteration, rather than explain, defend or answer.

We borrowed from these experiences to create our own feedback process. We use the same general principles, but our questions vary depending on the exercise or what feels useful in the moment. Throughout Part 3, you'll see examples of questions we ask.

THE PURPOSE of feedback is to be useful to the recipient.

Amy: *When I was 17, I studied at Uta Hagen's acting studio every Saturday. During class, we did many improv exercises. One of the most challenging was called, "Please and No." We were each assigned one of the words and restricted to only using that word. My word was "No." Then, we* *had to make up the backstory together and act out a 10-minute scene in front of the group using only our assigned word.*

My partner and I were completely off the mark in our delivery, and the teacher made sure we knew it. I never performed in class again.

I learned three things from that experience: The way feedback is given can encourage or discourage; words are not the only part of a conversation and maybe not even the most important part; and you have to practice even though it's improv.

What we've discovered is that sharing what we love about someone's work (vs. critiquing) creates a positive experience for the person giving the feedback as well as the one receiving it. Learning how to give feedback, particularly positive feedback, helps us all grow.

How We Do It

After each *Coaching with a Twist* conversation, we usually ask the coach: "What did you learn from that?" We used to ask, "What was that like for you?" but almost always got the response, "It was hard." So we learned to ask better questions.

Next we elicit learning from the client and then open it to the observers: "What did you notice that went well or was strong in the coaching?"

In the Introduction to Part 3, we share more details on our debriefing process. It's not necessary to do the debriefs in our instructions, though reflection is a key element in learning. If you don't have time, don't feel comfortable doing it, or just want to play, you might choose to wait until everyone has had a turn doing the exercise and then share reflections.

We once asked a participant what she was taking away from an exercise and she said, "I'll know later." Sometimes things need to sink in and often insights emerge over time. The impact of what we experience will have a life, just as our clients continue to process and integrate insight after leaving a coaching session.

Facilitator Challenge

If you're facilitating a group, it's important to also guide the feedback and handle situations where a participant's feedback might be hurtful or unfair to another. Participants will look to you as the facilitator to handle awkward situations and you need to address them.

In this type of situation, we want to be respectful of all parties and at the same time use it as a learning opportunity. Once during feedback after *Coaching with a Twist*, a student in the role of client said that their coach had shamed them. What we observed was that the client had a strong feeling and blamed the coach unfairly.

Despite the discomfort, knowing that one participant had likely hurt another, we needed to restore the safety in the group and set an example as to how to handle a challenging situation. Full disclosure: We did not handle this as we would now. We would have spent more time unpacking what was said with the client, coach and group.

Challenging situations are learning opportunities. In the case above, these include: 1) how to give useful feedback and, 2) how to help a client who is upset by something their coach may have done or said.

Addressing the first, how to give useful feedback: It's helpful to share what we feel, but we want to be careful not to attribute intent to another. In the example above, it would have been better for the client to say, "I felt shame in that moment" as opposed to, "You shamed me." Also, it's not necessarily a bad thing for shame to show up in a coaching session; it might be important for a client to explore.

Always approach giving feedback with humility. Focus on what the coach did well, what worked, and if they're open to it, share something specific and helpful. Helpful feedback includes clients and observers sharing specific reflections or questions offered by the coach. Or the client might share a specific moment that was helpful (e.g., when the client was spiraling and the coach interrupted to create a grounding moment).

Regarding the second opportunity, addressing disengagement in coaching, we want to recognize and repair the relationship. As coaches, when we notice a shift, disengagement or our client is upset, it can be helpful to reflect what we're noticing and inquire about it. For example, "I'm noticing a shift in your energy. If there's something I said that upset you, that was not my intent. Would you be willing to talk about it?" If the client says yes, we can unpack it together. One technique we might offer is OFNR (Observation, Feeling, Need, Request) from Non-Violent Communication.[3]

Requests for Specific Feedback

Sometimes a coach will ask for specific feedback like, "I'm working on asking open questions and want to know what you noticed about that." Or, "I'm curious if the agenda was clear." It's important to take specific notes of what the coach did or said during *Coaching with a Twist*. Just like with affirmations, the more specific and authentic the feedback is, the more useful it is to the recipient.

9

HUMOR

"A good laugh makes any interview, or any conversation, so much better."
— Barbara Walters

Unlike with the Groundlings, a professional improv comedy troupe from which many SNL cast members hail, *Improv for Coaches* does not have to be nonstop funny. Actually it doesn't have to be funny at all, though laughter in learning and coaching can be powerful. It can break tension and shift perspective. And sometimes it's a way to make life more tolerable.

As facilitators, we love to bring in humor when we can — in ways that are natural for us as individuals, acknowledging that we have different styles. Amy's style is silly and goofy, easily laughing at herself. Betsy's is more often one-liners, sarcasm or an exaggerated facial expression.

We enjoy some of the same comedy shows (e.g., *Lilyhammer*), but not all (Betsy likes *Trailer Park Boys*; Amy does not). Humor is different for everyone, so the pathways to draw it out can be different too. We include a variety of exercises that help participants discover what draws out their humor. Some people love storytelling and others like the more physical exercises. A favorite for some is World's Worst Coach (see Glossary of Improv Games).

You've no doubt heard that the secret to comedy is timing — whether in the telling of a joke or when to tell it. This applies not only to comedy performance, but also to using humor in our work as coaches and facilitators. Sometimes the best time for humor is when there is tension or discomfort in the room. A group of coach trainees once asked Betsy, "What do we do if the client starts crying near the end of the session?" Betsy responded, "You gotta make them cry earlier."

Humor can be deliberate or not. We often laugh at surprises, like when someone does something unexpected. It's also fun to watch people surprise themselves. We don't push for humor; we let it come naturally. But we've never had an *Improv for Coaches* session with no laughs.

We acknowledge that humor involves risk. It can feel scary when we don't know how an attempt at humor will be received. But as facilitators we can build trust within the group to give everyone a place to let their natural humor come out. We encourage participants to take the risk, acknowledging that risk-taking is a big part of this work. We also design for safety, trust and acceptance. Having everyone participate helps, as shared vulnerability increases acceptance and goodwill.

In the BNA world, there's a distinct element of wackadoodlery. We laugh at each other a lot and sometimes devolve into very unladylike behavior. In our work, Betsy is incredibly good with all the details and remembers (almost) everything. Amy has a tendency to space out periodically without realizing it. The result? Amy repeats something that Betsy has already said, which annoys Betsy and makes Amy laugh. When Betsy screws up, Amy loves it and always laughs because it makes her feel better about her own screw-ups. Betsy loves that Amy loves Betsy's screw-ups because it gives them a positive spin. Overall, we believe our mistakes make us more humble and hopefully, lovable. And remember, Improv Rule #4: There are no mistakes!

Okay there are mistakes but, as facilitators, we can reframe them. It helps when facilitators share their own mistakes or thoughts. For example, in the debrief after the word association warmup, Betsy asks, "Did anyone besides me think of a word and then think, 'I can't say that?'"

10

SIDE COACHING

Side coaching is when we provide real-time feedback or direction to someone while that person is coaching, allowing the coach to adjust on the spot. There are two ways we do this. Most often, we don't stop the conversation but gently interject with a suggestion. More rarely, we may pause an improvised coaching "scene" to have a short discussion.

Prior to side coaching, it's important to establish group norms. If you are a mentor coach or facilitator you might create a norm of side coaching without gaining permission before each coaching conversation. If you're a peer, we recommend asking permission before each coaching conversation. Just like with our clients, if a person grants permission, they're more likely to welcome our suggestions and in this case, interruption.

We might side coach if we see a coach struggling or to remind the coach of the skill we're focused on. For example, "What does the client want from the session?" or "Remember to use questions only."

We find it beneficial to wait a little while before interrupting a coaching conversation to allow the coach time to figure it out on their own, though we will step in if we think the coach needs help, or if they ask for it. However we side coach, we keep the focus on learning and experimenting.

There is learning in *everything*. If you stop a conversation to offer direction or support, be sure to send the coach back in to continue the conversation using the new skill or approach. The greatest learning comes from experiencing the shift.

In one instance, we stopped a coaching conversation to offer some feedback in the moment: "You're clearly listening to your client, and the deeper inquiry behind each closed question was right on. To increase the impact, take more time to formulate an open version of those questions." She then continued to coach, incorporating the suggestion.

The next day, she wrote: "I just wanted to share how impactful that session was for me — mostly around the point of my rushing to speak. As I've had some time to digest, I've noticed that I am 'rushing' a lot in my daily life. I chuckle as I write this because I teach meditation. I enjoy silence. I like turning my attention inward and allowing answers to reveal themselves. However, life has been a bit hectic lately and this feedback was helpful in noticing where I am."

11

CO-FACILITATION

You don't need two facilitators for *Improv for Coaches*. It can be facilitated by one person and was initially designed and facilitated by Betsy alone. But co-facilitating offers some unique advantages and we both prefer it. Some benefits are:

- It takes the pressure off both planning and executing.
- It's easier to keep on schedule because one facilitator can be monitoring the chat, setting up breakout rooms, or troubleshooting while the other is giving directions or leading a conversation with the group.
- It adds another perspective, point-of-view, style. Students remark that they appreciate the difference between us, enabling them to see that every coach is unique, giving them permission to be different too.

If you decide to go the co-facilitation route, choose your partner well, and work at maintaining the partnership and growing together. We began our co-facilitation journey by happy accident (Improv rule #4). Betsy was traveling to Scotland and was worried that spotty Wi-Fi might not allow her to teach her class. Amy offered to cover it. We both showed up and even though Betsy's Wi-Fi was working, we both stayed and wound up co-facilitating. It was so fun and successful that we continued to look for opportunities to work together.

If you're interested in co-facilitating, here are some insights from our partnership:

- **Like your mate.** This sounds obvious but we can't emphasize it enough. At the heart of co-facilitation is respect, honesty and trust. If you don't have those, co-facilitation can be arduous for the facilitators and the participants. Take the time to get to know one another and to enjoy the connection between the two of you before you take your show on the road.

- **Share how the partnership works in the room.** At the beginning of every course, we explain that one of the joys of co-facilitation is being able to rely on one another. We share that if one of us is leading, the other one might be taking care of something behind the scenes so if one of us looks distracted, it's because we're handling business. Betsy often adds that even when she's leading, she might look distracted because she's cross-eyed. So if it looks like she's not looking at you, it's because one eye is looking somewhere else.

- **Plan.** We like to be highly prepared for our offerings, but each in our own way. To make sure we're aligned before getting "on stage," we schedule time to create a lesson plan with all of the details we need to put on a great show, including agenda, timing for each agenda item, speaker assignments and all the information we want to convey. Practice delivering your lesson plan. While on Zoom, we communicate privately in the chat to check in and support one another throughout an offering. *Make sure you're private messaging and not messaging everyone.* After each session, we debrief with one another and incorporate any desired adjustments for future offerings.

- **Recognize the significance of the relationship.** We joke that we probably spend more time with one another (though nearly all virtual) than we do with our spouses. It's important to have time set aside regularly to celebrate what works well and to talk about what doesn't. We have very different personalities and over the years have had many conversations that could have been difficult because it was about things one of us was doing that didn't work for the other. Much to our relief, we're both open to feedback and work together to make change. We bring honesty, trust, commitment and a coaching mindset to the partnership.

- **Affirm each other.** Notice your partner's strengths and share that regularly — as you would with your clients.

We're intentional about spending time sharing and enjoying one another outside of work. All work and no play makes us cranky. A touch of laughter and time spent connecting makes us happy and relaxed.

∽

12

TIPS FOR RUNNING A GROUP IN ZOOM

For virtual groups, our platform of choice is Zoom. It has features that aren't available on other platforms, making it the most effective for an *Improv for Coaches* session. Be aware that in order to meet on Zoom for more than 40 minutes someone needs to have a professional (paid) account. (Full disclosure: Zoom does not sponsor us, although we would welcome it.)

While the hosts can do some things to adjust what people are seeing on their screens (e.g., spotlighting), each user determines if they're in gallery mode, if people are pinned, etc. So, you may need to help your participants sort out some settings on their end.

How to Make a "Circle" in Zoom

For many group exercises, a circle is necessary. If you are in an actual room with people, you can form a circle, whether standing or sitting, making it clear who follows who. If you're on Zoom, chances are everyone's "Brady Bunch" boxes are in a different order. Fortunately, it's possible to rearrange them.

To make our circle in Zoom, we put a list of names in the chat (usually in random order with the facilitator(s) going last), and the group is instructed on how to move the boxes so that everyone is looking at an identical screen. Technically, our Zoom circle is not really a circle but a series of rows.

To reorder the boxes, take the cursor into the box of the person who is at the top of the list, click on that box and drag it to the top left corner. Then take the box of the second person on the list and drag that one just to the right of the first person, and so on. This will not work if you don't go in order from top left to bottom right (i.e., don't try to move someone into the bottom right spot). If there are participants who are unable to do this, it's okay; they just need to know who they are following and who follows them. (Many people find that learning they can move the boxes alone is worth the price of the course.)

You'll also want to make sure that everyone has at least their first name visible. There's a setting in Zoom that may need to be checked by each individual in order for all names to be visible.

A Note about Chat

You can disable the chat feature in Zoom but we find the chat useful from time to time. During the first session, we ask participants not to use the chat, except when we specifically ask them to, as it's distracting and interferes with presence. The host can also change the chat setting to allow participants to chat with hosts and co-hosts only.

How to Pin

One Zoom skill that is useful is pinning, which is making one person's box large on your screen while all other boxes remain small. If you want to pin someone take your cursor into that person's box and click on the three dots in the upper right-hand corner, which will reveal a dropdown menu. Choose "Pin" and the person's box will become large and centered on your screen. This helps to focus on that one person. Participants can only pin one person at a time, though hosts and co-hosts can pin multiple people using "Spotlight." To unpin, click on "Remove pin." You can also click on "Gallery" view and everyone will return to the same size, though your pinned person will remain in the upper left corner.

Confidentiality

In keeping with confidentiality, we request that no humans other than participants be present during *Improv for Coaches* sessions. However, we have no problem (and indeed love it) when animals show up in the Zoom squares. One of the fun parts of Zoom is that we get to meet other people's pets – which would never happen in the office (at least not with the cats). These interlopers are cute, and we've never had a single one break confidentiality.

One time, a dog went beyond cute and actually helped with the coaching exercise. We were playing with skillfully interrupting and the coach got her dog to bark. She used that as a way to interrupt a client who was off on a tangent, and then said, "Excuse me, I'm just going to put the dog out ... I'm sorry about that. Where would be most helpful to go from here?"

Tech Challenges

On Zoom, there are audio defaults, settings and limitations that create challenges that would not happen in person. These issues apply to any coaching that's technology mediated and synchronous.

Micro delays due to internet connection make crosstalk more likely, making disruptive interruption more likely. The key to avoiding this is to leave more space in your coaching. Make sure the client is really finished talking before you speak. Unless of course, you are choosing to interrupt. (See Lesson Plan 4: Interrupting.)

Also, there is a default noise cancellation feature in Zoom that mutes sounds that you hear in your own environment. This has pros and cons. The pro is that others in the Zoom meeting don't hear ambient noise like leaf blowers, you clacking on your keyboard or the terrible music downstairs. The con is that it also blocks some intentional sounds. For example, during an improv exercise, you might make a seagull-like screech and others will hear nothing.

Zoom Bloopers

Zoom has a lot of cool features that can be useful and fun. One of the fun ones is what they call "Studio Effects." With Studio Effects, you can put lipstick, eyebrows, and facial hair on yourself without having to do any of this in real life. Sometimes it looks pretty real. Sometimes not so much.

When Betsy drinks from her white mug, her Zoom "lipstick" jumps to the front of the mug. Bonus points for noticing the stray Zoom eyebrow. These features are available in "Studio effects" in visual settings.

In late 2021, we met in person for the first time. We thought it would be a fun surprise for our students to see us in the same space. We got into an actual room and Zoom room together, which did not work out well.

For one thing, Betsy's Zoom lipstick kept jumping over to Amy's mouth, and was definitely *not* her color. And it also disturbed the equality of everyone having one square in gallery view on Zoom. We continued from separate rooms.

13

RUNNING A GROUP IN PERSON

In-person sessions offer some distinct advantages over virtual sessions. Assuming you are in a good space, distractions are less likely, internet speed doesn't matter, and group hugs are possible (with consent of course).

There is also a palpable energy that happens when we're physically in a room together. It allows for more of our bodies and energies to come into play, since we can see each other's whole bodies and feel each other's presence more directly. There's also no noise cancellation, so subtle sounds are more audible (for better and worse).

Designing the Space

An ideal setting will be quiet and comfortable, with open space to move around in and chairs for all participants.

Many exercises require a circle; however, for some exercises, such as when there is one client and many coaches, a horseshoe shape may be more appropriate.

During the 2-person *Coaching with a Twist* exercises, the coach and client will be on "stage" facing each other and observers will be in the audience. The facilitator(s) will also be "offstage."

Breaks

In our Zoom sessions, we do not usually take breaks as people have an opportunity to use the bathroom when they are off camera and (hopefully) muted during the *Coaching with a Twist* portion. In person, there is no off-camera, so you will need to schedule breaks.

Challenges

Things to consider for in-person meetings:

- They require a greater time commitment for most people as they must travel to and from the location.
- Transportation may be an additional expense.
- They may be more expensive due to a potential need to rent space.
- People in distant locations may be less able to join.
- If there's an outbreak of bird flu, Zoom might be a better choice.

"Performing" in person may be more anxiety provoking for some people since they can see everyone watching them. In our experience, this may provide a higher barrier to entry, but also greater rewards. Once an in-person group gets going, and group connection and a supportive environment has been created, participants will gain a greater level of confidence from having performed live in front of others.

PART III
LET'S PLAY!

"This moment is your curriculum."
– David Drake

INTRODUCTION TO PART 3

In this part, you'll find 12 lesson plans, each focused on a different coaching skill. Each lesson plan contains the following elements:

1. Discussion
2. Warmups
3. *Coaching with a Twist* Exercises
4. Debrief
5. Closing

Discussion

In the lesson plans below, we open each chapter with discussion of the skill. However, in an actual *Improv for Coaches* session, discussion of the skill is often incorporated at later points. That is, while we share the topic at the beginning of the session, we typically discuss the skill after debriefing relevant warm-up exercises. This enables participants to get right into the games and discover insights for themselves.

Depending on the level of the skill of the coaches in the room and the amount of time you have, it may be helpful to have a conversation about the skill in focus. In these discussions, we like to start by asking the group questions, eliciting their knowledge about the skill first and then filling in any gaps.

Every once in a while, we get someone who really wants to know what they're supposed to get out of an exercise before doing it. We encourage them to do the exercise first and if it's not clear after, we're happy to share our intentions. We've found that post-experience, the participants rarely need an explanation. Interestingly, what we intended as the purpose is usually more limited than what people actually get out of it. Someone in the group always has an insight beyond our own thinking.

Warmups

Each *Improv for Coaches* session begins with group warmups. While some people might consider warmups to be unimportant, frivolous or even inappropriate in a work setting, there is great value in the process and they should not be skipped.

The warmups provide the group with a transitional space to come together in connection, playfulness and presence. Participants may arrive exhausted, stressed or distracted. Warmups are an invitation to play and shift our energy as individuals and as a group.

They also provide a low stakes way to step into improv, helping participants see that they can do it. Last but not least, they're a lovely way to get to know each other. We sometimes start with a warmup exercise with no particular relation to the topic of the day. However, we choose at least one warmup designed to build skill related to the one that's emphasized in that session.

Coaching with a Twist **Exercises**

After warmups, each lesson plan includes a unique *Coaching with a Twist* exercise. These exercises are coaching conversations with a structure designed to enhance and focus experiential learning. By figuratively tying one hand behind the coach's back, we're concentrating the experience around a particular skill.

These exercises are about using experimental structures to learn while doing; they are not about completing a full coaching session in the allotted time. For our *Coaching with a Twist* exercises, we usually allot 5-to-7 minutes for each round. Feel free to change the length of the rounds so long as there is a designated timeframe and everyone can still participate. The 5-to-7-minute range may seem awfully short, but you would be amazed at how much can be accomplished in this amount of time.

Despite the shortened time frame, it remains true that all coaching sessions have a beginning, middle and end. Use the framework of a coaching session, which includes establishing an agenda (the agreement between the client and coach regarding the client's focus and desired outcome). Agenda is the element students are most likely to omit in these exercises and yet, focus and agenda are what makes a coaching session different from other kinds of conversations.

See where the session goes in the allotted time and bring the session, however short, to an intentional close. It's important to avoid forced planning, goal setting or problem solving, unless that is where the client wants to go in the available time. Trust that even a very short coaching conversation provides value through learning, growth and connection. One way for the coach to bring these short sessions to a natural close is to ask the client, "What did you learn?"

For those in the role of client, don't worry about being a 'good' or 'easy' client. There's no such thing as a bad client. The more real the client is, the better it is for the coach, as well as for the client's own learning. We never want our clients to try to please us as coaches. So if you're the client, relax and don't worry about the coach. If it's real play, be real. If it's role play, have fun acting!

We always use real play unless there's a specific reason not to. We use role play when it's in service to the coach's learning, for example, to practice dealing with red flags (e.g., a client expresses suicidal thoughts). In each lesson, we give instructions for the client that will make clear whether the exercise calls for real play or role play.

A Note on Red Flags. Red flags are defined as any concern for client health and safety (e.g., depression, suicidality, domestic violence, health condition). It's imperative that coaches know their scope of practice and when to refer clients to appropriate experts. While a referral may be appropriate, a red flag does not mean coaches must abruptly and automatically refer the client to another professional. Instead, the coach would explore with the client any red flag concern. After the scope and scale of the issue is understood, the coach can work with the client to design any next steps or plans, which may include seeking expert assistance. Of course, if the client is in imminent danger (e.g., having what appears to be a heart attack) the coach would interrupt and call 911. We recommend practicing these types of conversations with fellow coaches. For resources on coaching red flags, including a demo, please visit our website.[1]

Keeping It Real. Unless you're role playing, avoid pretending to have a past history. For example, "How'd you do with your goals from our last meeting?" If this were improv theater, that would be a great question for a client as it assumes a history of working together. However, if you've never coached this person before, you don't need a fake past. It takes away from the real conversation you're actually having. As coaches we have first sessions with many people. And coaching for the first time with someone is an important skill. Step in fresh. Yes they had a history before this session — but not with you. If you do know the person, we don't require you to leave out your knowledge and history. It can deepen the coaching.

Side Coaching. If you're a mentor coach or facilitator, you may create a norm of side coaching without gaining permission before each coaching conversation. If you're a peer group, it would be important to establish group norms around side-coaching and permissions. In our classes, as we share the *Coaching with a Twist* instructions for each *Improv for Coaches* session, we inform the participants that we may side coach by pausing the conversation and stepping in with guidance when it's in service to the coach. Even though we say this, we rarely interrupt, preferring coaches to figure out a way forward on their own.

Reasons we might interrupt include:

- Offering a gentle reminder if they've forgotten what the task is (e.g., "questions only").
- Asking if they would like help if they appear really stuck.
- Reminding the coach to clarify the agenda for the session.

For more on Side Coaching, see Part 1, sections on Side Coaching and Challenges.

Instructions for Observers

We invite you to embrace the opportunity to witness another coach's style by watching what the coach does, while trying not to think about what you might do instead.

Focus on what the coach does well. What were some gems that you might want to take with you into your coaching? Offer the coach affirmations. Be specific. Your feedback is not limited to the particular skill being explored but can be about any skill you notice. Here are some DON'Ts when giving feedback:

- Don't tell the coach what you think they did wrong.
- Don't tell the coach what you think they should have done.
- Don't tell the coach what you would've done instead.
- Don't give advice to the "client."

On Zoom, observers will mute their sound and stop their video and will not be visible during the *Coaching with a Twist* conversation. In person, the observers will be visible, with coach and client on "stage" facing each other and observers in the audience. The "performers" will want to "cheat out" a little so people can see their faces, much as people are arranged on talk or interview shows.

Debrief

Throughout the lessons, you'll find suggestions for debriefing after particular exercises. We debrief throughout the warm-up process, but not necessarily after every exercise. We do, however, debrief after each *Coaching with a Twist* conversation. This starts with the participants (coach and client) and then moves to the observers. After debriefing the coach and sometimes also the client, we invite the observers to share, "What did the coach do that was skillful?" After that, we share our feedback.

To support our ability to provide useful feedback, we write down strong reflections or questions that the coach used; the more specific we are with feedback, the more the recipient can take it in and decide what they think about it. Then, if the person is open to it, we might offer some possibilities for development and growth. Even here, it may be helpful instead to ask the individual what they see as areas for development. You may want to ask questions rather than offer your own feedback. (e.g., What would you do differently? What will you take into your coaching going forward?)

The participant in the role of the client should focus their feedback on their experience in the role of client as distinct from critiquing the coach or talking about the substance of their coaching session. From this vantage point, they will experience the impact of different choices on the part of the coach and will gain insight into the experience of clients. Coaches may wonder how something landed and it's helpful that the client is right there to check in with during the debrief.

For more on feedback, see "How to Give Feedback" in Part 2.

Closing the Session

Just as coaches typically close each individual coaching session by eliciting client learning and takeaways, we do the same in *Improv for Coaches*. It's important to plan enough time for this so that each person in the group can share.

Session Structure and Timing

In general, the way we lay out a two-hour session with eight participants looks like this:

- 45 minutes for warmups
- 1 hour for *Coaching with a Twist* exercises
- 15 minutes for learning and integration (i.e., debrief and closing)

Throughout the rest of the book, you'll see some repetition from lesson plan to lesson plan. We did this so that each lesson plan can stand alone. While there is replication in structure, there are meaningful differences, such as in the instructions and debrief questions.

LESSON PLAN 1: SUCCINCTNESS

We've all heard somebody tell a long-winded tale and thought, "Get to the f**king point." Excess verbiage is a barrier to clear communication and good coaching. We may struggle to convey our exact meaning or to find the right words for things, but we rarely need all the words we use.

Brevity is a key skill in communication. Express what's important with clarity and leave plenty of space for your client. In coaching, succinctness contributes to:

- Presence
- Trust
- Rapport
- Clarity
- Client autonomy
- More space for the client

In this lesson, the focus is on getting to the essence of what we're trying to communicate. And we think you'll find that you can effectively help your clients move forward with a lot less story (on everyone's part). The client already knows the story and the coach probably doesn't need to.

Here are a few examples of questions and reflections improved by succinctness:

> **Long-winded coach question:** So based on what you just said, I want to ask how you're feeling right now? What are you thinking you want to feel in the future? What would that look like?
> **Succinct coach question:** How do you want to feel?
>
> **Long-winded coach reflection:** You're feeling like you want to maybe go into the future with a clear plan of what you want, perhaps a vision of how to feel and how to act, which would be really helpful to figure out.
> **Succinct coach reflection:** You want a vision and clear plan.

SUGGESTED WARMUPS

WARMUP 1: Mirror
This exercise, which you can also find in the Glossary of Improv Games, is a gift from the improv theater world.[1] We have added reflection and learning prompts that focus on relevance to coaching.

STRUCTURE
This exercise is completed in pairs, which requires breakout rooms for virtual delivery. Following the paired portion, the group comes back together for a full group version of the exercise.

Instructions

- Each pair: choose the first leader and follower.
- Keep your eyes open and face your partner like you're looking into a mirror. The leader moves their body, limbs and face. The follower mirrors the leader as if they were a mirror image. Tip: Maintain eye contact.
- After about two minutes, switch roles so that the leader becomes the follower and the follower becomes the leader.
- After another couple of minutes, shift to having no leader. In this portion, each person follows the other. With no leader, things will tend to slow down as you each try to mirror exactly what you see in the other.

When everyone has returned from breakouts to the larger "circle," do one more round with the full group in which there is no leader. Everyone should try to follow the others. The goal is to become so present and in sync that the whole group is doing exactly the same thing. It's very hard to achieve this, but a lot of fun to try. For those who do group coaching or facilitate groups, this is a great way to practice attuning to a group and everybody in it.

Debrief

- What did you notice?
- Did you prefer leading or following? Or when no one is leading?
- What did you notice about the connection with your partner?
- What does this have to do with coaching?

As with all coaching questions, there is no right or wrong answer, just an opportunity for self-reflection.

WARMUP 2: Three-Word Story

This exercise, which you can also find in the Glossary of Improv Games, is a gift from the improv world.

Structure

In this exercise, the group will tell a story together, with each person speaking only three words at a time before moving to the next person to continue the story. We use the general structure of a fairy tale or children's story, starting with 'Once upon a time...' and ending with 'The moral of the story is....' This exercise is followed by a group debrief.

Instructions

- Create a circle.
- Ask the group for a theme for the story. The theme can be a combination of more than one suggestion.
- When the group is ready, open the story with: "Once upon a time."
- Each person takes a turn adding to the story by contributing three words. Punctuation is implied verbally using inflection.
- When the story has gone on long enough, someone will say, "And the moral of the story is..." and the group will complete that sentence, bringing the story to an end.

Example

Story Theme: Bunnies in a Bakery

Person 1: Once upon a
Person 2: time there was
Person 3: a bunny named
Person 4: Boo Boo Bunny.
Person 5: His friends made
Person 6: carrot cake for

Person 7: his birthday party.
Person 8: It was the
Person 1: worst cake ever.
Person 2: Boo Boo decided
Person 3: to burn the
Person 4: bakery down and
Person 5: build a bank
Person 6: in its place.
Person 7: His friends did
Person 8: not want him
Person 1: to put the
Person 2: baked goods in
Person 3: the vault. Instead,
Person 4: they wanted him
Person 5: to share all
Person 6: the goods with
Person 7: rabbits from labs
Person 8: who were very
Person 1: blind from the
Person 2: shampoo testing. They
Person 3: all agreed to
Person 4: start a new
Person 5: world. The moral
Person 6: of the story
Person 7: is make sure
Person 8: you give cake
Person 1: that is delicious
Person 2: to all bunnies
Person 3: everywhere. The End.

Debrief

- What did you notice?
- What does this have to do with coaching?

COACHING WITH A TWIST: **3-Word Coaching**

This exercise is adapted for coaching from three-word scenes from the improv world. This is sometimes done with different numbers of words like two or even just one.

Three-Word Coaching is not a method of coaching but, rather, a method of *learning*. For example, in this lesson, some coaches thought we were suggesting that they should do 3-Word Coaching with their clients. That is not our intention. We designed this to help you discover the value of being succinct. Having said that, some of our students have offered 3-Word Coaching to their clients and have had great success. So you never know.

STRUCTURE

In this *Coaching with a Twist*, both the coach and client, in turn, use only three words at a time. The words do not need to form a grammatically correct sentence. The point is to communicate the essence of what you are trying to share.

In most exercises in this book, the client shows up as any client would in a normal coaching session (i.e. no restrictions). In this exercise, the client is asked to adhere to the three-word limit.

INSTRUCTIONS

- **Participants:** 1 coach, 1 client
- **Time frame:** 5 - 7 minutes of coaching
- **Coach and Client:** Each uses only three words per exchange.
- **Client:** Choose an area of focus that is authentic (i.e. real play versus role play)
- **Coach:** Use reflections and open questions (vs. closed). Use the framework of a coaching session, which includes

establishing an agenda (the agreement between the client and coach regarding the client's focus and desired outcome). Keep the conversation real. Don't pretend you have a past or future with this client — unless you really do.
- **Facilitator/Timekeeper:** Cue the coach after 5 - 6 minutes to bring it to a close.
- **Observers:** If on Zoom, turn off camera and audio during the coaching, and avoid writing in the chat as this can distract the coach and client.

Debrief

Elicit the coach's and then the client's experience of using only three words.

- What did you learn from that?
- What was useful in being restricted to just three words?

Observers:

- What did you notice?
- What did the coach do that was skillful and effective?
- What moments stood out for you?

Closing the Session

After everyone has had a turn to serve as either coach or client, invite each person in the group to share what they are taking away from the session.

∽

LESSON PLAN 2: QUESTIONS

As coaches, we work with clients to generate insight, learning and growth. One of the key skills to accomplish this is asking effective questions. These are usually open and typically begin with *how* or *what* thus inviting a client to think beyond a one-word answer (often yes or no).

There is no list of pre-determined "powerful" questions. Creating questions is all in the moment; whether they are powerful depends on the particular client and conversation.

> **Betsy:** *I once coached a session in which the question, "What do you love about basketball?" opened up everything for that client. But that's not a question I have ever asked any other client.*

You will likely not know which questions will be powerful until the client responds. Sometimes their response is silence and thought. Sometimes they'll say, "That's a great question!" Sometimes it's most powerful to repeat back a question the client asked. For example, a client might say, "What do I really **want**?" And the coach responds, "What **do** you really want?"

What makes for a strong coaching question?

For one, questions should generally be open, concise and asked one at a time.

If you're a coach who stacks questions — i.e., asks a question and then re-words it, tries again with better words or metaphors, in other words, asks multiple questions in a row because you think your question wasn't clear, or asks three questions in a row hoping one of them lands — practice asking just one question and let it land. If the client doesn't understand your question, they'll tell you. We don't have to word questions perfectly to have an impact.

It's helpful to incorporate the client's words, metaphors or beliefs into the questions we ask. A useful or client-centered question is one that's in service of the client, rather than in service of the coach's curiosity. For example, when we ask for details about something because we're curious, the client already knows all the details, so this doesn't serve them. Tying back to the earlier lesson on succinctness (see Lesson Plan 1): We don't need all the details to coach well.

> **Coach-centered curiosity:** What happened?
> **Client-centered curiosity:** What did you learn from that experience?

Sometimes, a coach will ask a question and the client answers a different question. The coach might think that the client didn't answer the question, but what the client heard the coach ask may be what they needed to answer. On the flip side, we've also heard clients say, "Did I answer your question?" This is an opportunity for the coach to clarify the coaching relationship by reminding the client that it's not about answering the coach's question, it's about what's useful to the client.

Take your time. Give yourself space to think about what would actually be helpful to ask at this moment; consider options and then choose a direction. If you're stumped on where to go, remember that you can always ask the client — your partner — "What do you want to explore here?" or "What would be a useful question to ask?" or "Where do you want to go from here?"

"Why" Questions

There's an unwritten rule that we should avoid questions that begin with *why*. It's not 100%, but *why* questions have limited use in coaching. Questions that begin with why can seem judgmental (e.g. "Why did you do that?"), which diminishes rapport between the coach and client. These kinds of questions are not usually helpful. But "Why is this important to you?" could be helpful.

Keep in mind that you could frame most *why* questions as *what* questions. For example, instead of "Why is this important to you?" you might ask "What's important to you about this?"

Another consideration with *why* questions is tone. How you ask a question can be as important as the words you use. (Alas, we cannot demonstrate this in a book.)

Closed Questions

We generally avoid closed questions because they tend to be narrowing and often directive. For the most part, closed questions limit the client to a yes or no answer. And most closed questions could be reworded to be open.

There are some less obvious forms of closed questions such as multiple-choice. By listing multiple choices and then asking the client to choose, you are closing down options and thereby leading. For example, by offering a specific menu (such as "Do you want A or B?" or "You mentioned three topics, which one of those do you want to focus on today?"), you're limiting the client's choice. Maybe they really want to talk about something not listed, or maybe there's an overarching theme that would be missed by asking to choose just one. Instead of asking if the client wants to focus on A or B, you might ask the client, "You mentioned A and B; what do you want to focus on?" You might also offer, "Perhaps there's a common thread between them or something else altogether."

However, there are no absolutes in coaching. Sometimes, a closed question can be powerful. Here are some situations when closed questions might be beneficial:

- **Challenging Self-Judgment:** "Is that true?" might be useful when challenging a client's limiting belief.
- **Assessing Readiness:** Questions such as: "Are you ready?" or "Do you want this?" can help a client clarify readiness or commitment. However, we can also use a version that's open, such as "How ready are you?"
- **Clarifying:** In an instance where there's a red flag (a warning signal or sign of any safety or wellness concern on the part of either client or coach that may suggest needs outside of our scope of practice), the coach may want to know if the client has consulted a doctor. Though, even in this case, we might be able to ask this in a more open way: "Who have you discussed this with?" or "What other support do you have around this?" or "What are your thoughts about consulting with a medical provider?"
- **Addressing Suicidality:** If the client has shared or you suspect suicidal ideation, it's important to discuss this and address it clearly. You may need to ask, "Do you have thoughts about killing yourself?" "Do you have a plan?" (We share resources on coaching red flags, including how and when to refer to qualified professionals, on our website.[1])

Don't Interrogate Your Clients

As a coach, you want to balance questions with reflections. Reflections contribute to clients feeling heard and respected. Some coach training emphasizes questions more than reflections. Other training emphasizes using reflections more than questions. We think the balance depends on the client and what serves that particular conversation.

SUGGESTED WARMUPS

The next two warmups come from the world of improv theater. We've adapted them for our purposes by following them with the discussion question: "What does this have to do with coaching?" We find these warmups helpful for sharpening presence, listening skills, and freeing imagination — all while having fun.

WARMUP 1: Last Letter

<u>Structure</u>
This exercise involves the whole group.

<u>Instructions</u>

- Create a circle.
- The facilitator is last in the lineup.
- The first person says any word they choose.
- The next person in the circle says a word that begins with the last letter of the first person's word.
- The next person says a word that begins with the last letter of the second person's word, etc.

We typically do at least 3 rounds, but you can choose however many you like. With a smaller group you may want to do more rounds.

<u>Example</u>

- chart
- tango

- octopus
- scatter
- rancid
- dastardly
- yodel

Note for Facilitators: Sometimes, a person's word doesn't start with the last letter of the previous word. Most of the time, people just go with it and often learn from that. Sometimes our clients answer a different question from the one we asked, and that's fine. The only time we would interrupt is if a number of people in a row don't do the exercise as expected, in which case we remind the group that we're playing Last Letter.

∼

WARMUP 2: Word Association (aka Free Association)

<u>Structure</u>
This exercise involves the whole group, continuing on from the previous warm-up (Last Letter).

<u>Instructions</u>

- The group creates a circle or continues the circle from the previous warmup.
- The facilitator is last in the lineup.
- The first person says a word.
- The next person in the circle says the very first word that comes to mind.
- The next person says the first word that comes to mind, based on the word from the person immediately before them, etc.

We typically do at least 3 rounds. With a smaller group you may want to do more rounds.

Example

- Acorn
- Tree
- Family
- Feud
- Hatfields

Debrief

- What did you notice?
- If you had a preference for last letter or word association, what was it and why?
- What does this have to do with coaching?

WARMUP 3: Question Story

Story is a common improv structure that you'll also find in the Glossary of Improv Games, along with its many variations. This is a version that we adapted for this lesson.

Structure

In Question Story, the group builds a story together by each person asking a question in turn. This exercise involves the whole group. Unlike the 3-Word Story exercise in Lesson 1, this version does not start with "Once upon a time," nor end with "The moral of the story is____."

Instructions

- Form a circle (or stay in your circle if you have one from the above warmups).
- Get a topic from the group.
- Imagine this like a children's book with each question being a page, taking the reader on a journey.
- The story begins with the first person asking a question about the topic.
- Each person takes a turn adding to the story by contributing a question that somehow moves the story forward. No reflections or statements are allowed.
- Unless someone else has brought the story to a natural end, when the story has gone on long enough, the facilitator brings it to a close, using a question, of course.

Example

TOPIC: The New Cat

Who are you little kitty?
What has brought you here?
Why are your little feet so dirty?
How did you get so scruffy?
Where's your momma?
Are you all alone?
What makes you so good at making biscuits?
Would you like some milk to go with them?
Would you like to nap after finishing your milk?
Would you like to jump in my lap?
What if you stayed here forever?
Would you like that?
How would it feel to wake up snuggled next to me?
Do you like the name Burt?
Could it be that you're a Sally?
What's that you say?

You want to stay?
Why do cats always vomit on the rug?

Debrief

- What did you notice?
- What did you like about that?
- What does this have to do with coaching?

Coaching with a Twist: Questions

Structure

In this *Coaching with a Twist* exercise, the coach is restricted to only asking questions. There are no restrictions for the client.

Instructions

- **Participants:** 1 coach, 1 client
- **Time frame:** 5 - 7 minutes of coaching
- **Client:** Choose an area of focus that is authentic (i.e., real play versus role play)
- **Coach:** Keep your questions open as much as possible. Use the framework of a coaching session, which includes establishing an agenda (the agreement between the client and coach regarding the client's focus and desired outcome). While this exercise restricts the coach from reflecting, helpful questions are based on deep listening, thus, in a sense, what might be reflected is implicit in the question. For example: Client says, "I feel really bad about the conversation but I don't want to take all the blame." The coach might ask: "What part do you want to own?" Resist the temptation to turn a reflection into a question by combining them. For instance, using the example

above: "You feel bad but don't want to take all the blame; what part do you want to take?" Keep the conversation real. Don't pretend you have a past or future with this client — unless you really do.
- **Facilitator/Timekeeper:** Cue the coach after 5 - 6 minutes to bring it to a close.
- **Observers:** If on Zoom, turn off camera and audio during the coaching, and avoid writing in the chat as this can distract the coach and client.

Debrief

Elicit the coach's experience of using only questions.

- What did you learn from that?
- What was useful in being restricted to questions only?

Client:

- How did it feel to be coached with only questions?

Observers:

- What did you notice?
- What did the coach do that was skillful and effective?
- What moments stood out for you?

Closing the Session

After everyone has had a turn to serve as either coach or client, invite each person in the group to share what they are taking away from the session.

∽

LESSON PLAN 3: REFLECTIONS

Reflections are statements that convey your understanding of what the client is saying or feeling, without judging, interpreting or advising.

Skillful reflection results from deep listening and presence. Sharing our understanding of what the client is trying to communicate helps to clarify understanding, deepen learning and express empathy. When a client knows they're being heard without judgment, reflections build rapport, trust and safety.

The purpose of reflections is to move the conversation forward. In addition to reflecting what a client says, we can reflect energy, emotions, tone, body language, patterns, discrepancy, ambivalence, beliefs, values, strengths and more. A reflection is an offering to your client for them to agree, disagree or reformulate for their learning and growth.

If you hang onto your reflections as truth, you are in coach agenda as opposed to being client-centered. When you reflect, it doesn't matter if you're "right." What you're going for is your best understanding of what the client is trying to communicate. You're giving the client the opportunity to clarify, not for you, but for them.

If you're uncertain whether you understood the client, ask for clarification before reflecting.

After offering a reflection, resist the urge to follow it with, "Did I get that right?" This question makes it about the coach rather than being a prompt for the client to reflect.

Leave space for the client to process what you've said. After a powerful reflection, the client might not say anything immediately. They might need to take it in. Support your client by holding space and silence.

Sometimes a client will say, "Oh, yeah, you totally have it!" This may build rapport in the moment; however, you might not be going deep enough if during the course of a coaching session, your client repeatedly says, "Right." or "Yes, exactly." This may be a signal that the conversation isn't moving forward.

The umbrella of reflections includes affirmations, simple and complex reflections, and summaries.

- **Affirmations** help to build a person's confidence in their ability to change. They may be a reflection of a client's strengths, values, desires, vision, qualities, achievements. Affirmations should be genuine and specific, allowing the client to assess if it resonates. They are distinct from praise or cheerleading, which is a form of judgment (even if positive). (For more on Affirmations, check out Motivational Interviewing & Beyond: Affirmations and Praise.[1])

- **Reflections** can be either simple or complex. Simple reflections (repeating or rephrasing what the person said with little or no alteration) can be useful in highlighting key words. More often, coaches use complex reflections, to highlight ambivalence, dissonance, emotions, values, energy, tone, body language, language, patterns, beliefs, etc. One type of complex reflection is the double-sided reflection (e.g. on the one hand ____, and on the other hand _____). Complex reflections may reflect things that are not said, as well as patterns and themes noticed over time. We can even open a conversation with a reflection as we take in the person in front of us. (For more, see *Motivational Interviewing, 4th edition.*[2])

- **Summaries** ensure shared understanding and reinforce key points made by the client. They should be used sparingly. If we summarize everything the client says, we're repeating information they already know, using time that could be better spent exploring new territory. Summaries can be helpful when a client gives a lot of information at once, for example, during the initial part of the conversation, when it could be helpful to highlight some key points as you move toward creating an agenda. Some coaches like to summarize for the client, for example, ending the session by summarizing the client's plan; instead, try inviting the client to summarize for themselves. Often, the client's summary will be different from the coach's. Keep the invitation open, not restricting the client to summarizing only their plan. Learnings and takeaways are also important.

SUGGESTED WARMUPS

WARMUP 1: Made-up Yoga Poses

<u>Structure</u>
This exercise involves the whole group.

<u>Instructions</u>

- One member of the group makes up an original yoga pose and names it. The participant can add "asana" to the name of the pose for added fun (e.g., funky-chicken-asana). Anything goes here. Silliness is encouraged. Note that a pose can include movement. If on Zoom, you are still free to stand up and use more than just your head and shoulders.
- Share the name of the pose and demonstrate it for the group.
- Everyone in the group then does the pose.
- The person who made up that pose chooses the next group member.
- This person offers an affirmation to the person before them. The affirmation should be coach-consistent as opposed to cheerleading or coach judgment. (e.g., instead of saying something like, "I love that pose" or "Now I feel great," the affirmer shares a strength, value, energy or quality: "You showed creativity and humor in your choice of *insert yoga pose name*.") After the affirmation is offered, this person will make up a new yoga pose, name it, demonstrate it, and the group will then do that pose.
- Continue until everyone has gone, closing the circle with the first yoga poser offering an affirmation to the last.

Debrief

- What did you notice?

WARMUP 2: Reflection Circle

Structure
This exercise involves the whole group.

Instructions

- One coach chooses another participant and shares a reflection, without the participant having said anything. It could be about the way this person has shown up in the moment, or a strength or value that person has exhibited, or even something in the client's environment.
- The receiver takes in the reflection but does not respond verbally.
- The recipient then chooses the next person to offer a reflection to and assumes the role of coach.
- This continues until everyone has both reflected and received a reflection.

Debrief

- What did you notice about reflecting in this way?
- What did you notice as the recipient of the reflection?

WARMUP 3: Reflection Batting Practice
With gratitude to MINT[3] Trainer Suzanne Alfandari.[4]

Structure

This involves members of the group responding in no particular order. The facilitator will offer a client statement and different members of the group will offer reflections. There can be many reflections for each client statement.

Instructions

- The facilitator offers one of the following client statements:
    - I've tried everything. I just don't think it's possible.
    - I had the best weekend. I was with my kids and we laughed so hard.
    - I can't stop yawning.
    - My team is a mess. We're never going to have our presentation ready in time.
    - I've had this big loss and I don't know what to do. I'm just spinning.
    - **Make up your own - or ask other participants to share client statements that have stumped them.**
- Multiple participants offer reflections, one at a time. There is no limit to how many different reflections can be offered. Be creative. Take chances.
- Repeat with other client statements. We recommend at least four rounds.

Debrief

- What did you notice?
- What was useful about that exercise?

Coaching with a Twist: Reflections

Structure

In this *Coaching with a Twist*, the coach is restricted to offering reflections only. Because of the challenge of setting an agenda without any questions, we allow one question during the coaching. There are no restrictions for the client.

Instructions

- **Participants:** 1 coach, 1 client
- **Time frame:** 5 - 7 minutes of coaching
- **Client:** Choose an area of focus that is authentic (i.e., real play versus role play).
- **Coach:** Offer reflections only. It is possible to do it with no questions, but due to the challenge of creating a clear agreement, you're allowed one question. Don't waste it on, "How are you?" Rather, use it to move the conversation forward. For example, you might ask a question to ascertain or clarify the client's agenda or to elicit client insights. Use the framework of a coaching session, which includes establishing an agenda (the agreement between the client and coach regarding the client's focus and desired outcome). Keep the conversation real. Don't pretend you have a past or future with this client — unless you really do.
- **Facilitator/Timekeeper:** Cue the coach after 5 - 6 minutes to bring it to a close.
- **Observers:** If on Zoom, turn off camera and audio during the coaching, and avoid writing in the chat as this can distract the coach and client.

Debrief

Elicit the coach's experience of using reflections only.

- What did you learn from that?
- What was useful in being restricted to just reflections?

Client:

- How did it feel to be coached with mostly reflections?

Observers:

- What did you notice?
- What did the coach do that was skillful and effective?
- What moments stood out for you?

Closing the Session

After everyone has had a turn to serve as either coach or client, invite each person in the group to share what they are taking away from the session.

LESSON PLAN 4: INTERRUPTING

In this lesson, we cover interrupting, including when it is in service to the client, when it is not (e.g., coach agenda) and, when it *is* in service to the client, how to interrupt skillfully.

Useful Interruption

Consider interrupting when a client is:

- ruminating or repeating stories or information.
- off on a tangent, spinning or disconnected.
- stuck in sustain talk.[1]
- off topic or agenda.
- without an agenda or the agenda needs clarifying.
- nearing the end of the session and you want to ensure the client can use the remaining time most beneficially.

It might also be important to interrupt if there is a red flag. However, having a reason to interrupt does not mean we abruptly do so right then. Timing is important.

Disruptive Interruption

Times we would not want to interrupt include:

- The client is a verbal processor and is working through something.
- The client is thinking.
- The coach has an idea to share (coach agenda).
- The coach wants to go in a different direction (coach leading).
- The client is writing notes.
- The client is experiencing deep emotion.

How to Skillfully Interrupt

Determining that interrupting is in service is just the first step. Then we must actually do it. Interrupting can be very uncomfortable, and many of us have been taught that it is rude. In fact, interrupting is part of our job as coaches.

Done skillfully, interrupting will reconnect a client to the coach, to the conversation and, most importantly, to themself. If a client is caught up in story or overwhelming thoughts or feelings, being interrupted may come as a relief. Skillful interruption can be practiced and we think this lesson is a great way to do it. Be bold and experience the pay off.

Interrupting skillfully takes place in two parts: first, get the client's attention and second, redirect. If you come straight in with your redirect, there's a good chance the client will not hear the beginning of what you say because they are still talking or are focused on their own thoughts. It may also feel rude, like you are talking over them (crosstalk).

By getting the client's attention first, verbally or with body language, we are able to support that client through redirection, be it a reflection, a question or a reframe.

Examples

- John...I just want to check in with you...
- Can I interrupt for a moment? (*client affirms*). We have about 20 minutes left, and I just want to be sure we're using it in a way that serves you well. How would you like to use the time?
- (*Coach leans in.*) Wow! That's a lot. Would it be okay if I summarized what I'm hearing to make sure I'm understanding?
- Do you mind if I jump in here? You mentioned you're feeling ungrounded today. What would help you feel grounded?
- If we're together, there may be times that I'll interrupt you. Here's why... (*Then co-create with the client what would work best in regard to interruptions. This may be part of establishing norms with clients and may even be something you do when initially contracting with a client.*)
- With an eye on the clock, could I jump in? (*Client agrees.*) What are you taking away from this conversation so far?

We recommend paying attention to the sensations in your body (e.g., an uncomfortable feeling in your chest) that may be telling you that where the conversation is going is not helpful and that you need to step in. Allow that feeling to inform you, and then thoughtfully interrupt.

While this lesson is focused on intentionally interrupting to support your client, we want to acknowledge that sometimes interruptions happen that are beyond our control. Some examples are: a power or internet outage on either end of the conversation; an intrusion of another person into the space; the coach has a coughing fit. In such cases, part one (getting the client's attention) has already happened. So the focus is on reconnection and coming back into presence with each other. Depending on the nature of the disruption, this may include an apology or inquiry about the safety or well-being of the client. You will need to address the disruption, reestablish rapport and come back to the client's agenda.

SUGGESTED WARMUPS

WARMUP 1: Counting

This exercise is a gift from the improv universe.

STRUCTURE

This exercise involves the whole group. If on Zoom, be sure that everyone is on camera and unmuted. Virtual play requires that all participants have a solid, high-speed internet connection.

In Counting, the group counts from 1 to at least 10 and ideally far beyond. We once had a group (of 8) get to more than 100.

INSTRUCTIONS

- The facilitator starts by saying, "One."
- Anyone can say the next number. There's no order to who goes when, but a person cannot say 2 numbers in a row.
- If two people speak at the same time, the group goes back to 1.
- Keep going until the group gets to 10, but don't stop there. See how high you can go.

It sounds easier than it is!

DEBRIEF

- What did you notice?
- What does this have to do with coaching?

Lesson Plan 4: INTERRUPTING | 87

WARMUP 2: Interruption Circle

STRUCTURE
This exercise involves the whole group.

INSTRUCTIONS

- Set up Zoom or live circle.
- The first person in the circle is the rambler. The second person is the interrupter.
- The rambler continues until interrupted. Ideally, think of something you have a lot of story about — things you're ambivalent about are often good candidates; if you're not a naturally chatty person, channel your chattiest client or friend.
- After the rambler has gone on for a bit, the second person interrupts them.
- Then the interrupter becomes the rambler, and the third person becomes the interrupter. When you're the rambler, your topic or story doesn't have to connect to what the previous rambler was talking about.
- This continues until everyone has been both rambler and interrupter, ending with the first person (rambler) interrupting the last person in the circle.

DEBRIEF

- What did participants notice in the roles of rambler and interrupter?
- What was it like to interrupt?
- What was it like to be interrupted?

Discussion

Skillful vs Disruptive Interruption
Discuss when it is in service to interrupt and when it is not.

Ways to Interrupt
How do you interrupt?

Brainstorm some new ways you could interrupt.

If you're facilitating, invite the participants to share how they do it or brainstorm new ideas together.

The Two Parts of Interrupting

1. Get the client's attention.
2. Offer a helpful redirect.

WARMUP 3: Skilled Interruption Circle
Repeat the Interruption Circle from Warmup 2, but this time include the two parts of interruption. The rambler will be a chatty client and the interrupter will be coach.

Coaching with a Twist: Interrupting

Structure
In this *Coaching with a Twist,* the coach is challenged to interrupt. The client will be in role play as their task is to provide the need for interruption; however, the topic can be real.

Because the focus of this *Coaching with a Twist* is on interrupting, we find that a little prep beforehand makes it easier for the coach to stay focused on the coaching rather than on dreaming up new ways to get the client's attention. Before starting the coaching conversations, each participant writes down five different ways to get the client's attention. This is for each coach's personal use — don't share with the group. Go for silly and creative. This is the play part — don't be limited by what you would actually do in a coaching session. Some favorite examples from past sessions include clapping a (non-existent) mosquito; disappearing below the screen; having a dog bark; hysterical laughter; turning off the video. Making this list enables the coach to focus on being present in the conversation; by not spending focus or energy thinking up novel ways to get the client's attention, the coach can pay more attention to the timing of interruptions and useful redirection.

INSTRUCTIONS

- **Participants:** 1 coach, 1 client
- **Time frame:** There is no time restriction as it ends whenever the coach has interrupted for the 5th time.
- **Client:** Using ROLE PLAY, clients should be VERY chatty, using things like sustain talk, tangents and rumination. We recommend choosing a real topic about which you have ambivalence or a lot of story. If this is challenging for you as yourself, feel free to channel a client or other person who fits this bill.
- **Coach:** Interrupt in five different ways. Try to interrupt only at times when it would be helpful for the client. After getting the client's attention using a creative method, offer a real redirect. Use the framework of a coaching session, which includes establishing an agenda (the agreement between the client and coach regarding the client's focus and desired outcome). Keep the conversation real. Don't pretend you have a past or future with this client — unless you really do.

- **Facilitator/Timekeeper:** Count the number of times the coach interrupts and end the session after the client responds to the fifth interruption.
- **Observers:** If on Zoom, turn off camera and audio during the coaching, and avoid writing in the chat as this can distract the coach and client.

Technical issues that may affect this exercise

On Zoom, there are audio defaults, settings and limitations that create challenges to interrupting that don't happen when we are face-to-face. These issues do not just apply to interrupting, but to any coaching that is technology-mediated.

Micro delays due to internet connection make crosstalk more likely, which makes disruptive interruption more likely. The key to avoiding these interruptions is to leave more space in your coaching. Make sure the client is really finished talking before you speak. Unless, of course, you want to interrupt.

When you want to interrupt, be aware that Zoom's default audio setting suppresses noise, so if you try to get your client's attention using sound, *you* will hear the sound (e.g., screaming or chicken squawking), but the client may not hear you. There's no way for you to know whether you were heard, except that you won't see a response. If you clap, say 'Wow!' or do something else audible and the other person doesn't accept the interruption, assume they didn't hear you and try something else. However, it's possible that you were heard and the other person chose not to respond.

You can change your Zoom audio settings to minimize this issue. This will be particularly helpful for group Zoom meetings. If you want to try it, look under Audio Settings, scroll down to "Audio profile" and choose "Original sound for musicians." This is particularly helpful for this lesson. Remember to put it back to the default afterward or people will hear you clacking on your keyboard as well as other background noise.

Debrief
Elicit the coach's experience of interrupting.

- What did you learn from that?

Client:

- How did it feel to be interrupted?

Observers:

- What did you notice?
- What did the coach do that was skillful and effective?
- What moments stood out for you?

Closing the Session
After everyone has had a turn to serve as either coach or client, invite each person in the group to share what they are taking away from the session.

LESSON PLAN 5: FOCUS AND AGENDA

Getting to focus and agenda (co-creating the coach-client agreement) is one of the most crucial and challenging parts of coaching. What makes a coaching conversation different from other conversations is that coach and client come to a clear agreement as to what the client wants to explore within a session, what the client's true underlying goal or desire is, and what the client wants to achieve during the session. With this clearly understood, the coach can help guide the client through the conversation to finding their own answers.

The International Coaching Federation dedicates an entire competency to this process. Competency 3 reads: "Establishes and Maintains Agreements: Partners with the client ... to create clear agreements about the coaching relationship, process, plans and goals. Establishes agreements for the overall coaching engagement as well as those for each coaching session."

Leadership and mentor coach Jonathan Reitz offers the TOMMY acronym to simplify the process for an individual session:[1]

- **T: Topic** (What do you want to talk about?)
- **O: Outcome** (What will you have when we're done?)

Lesson Plan 5: FOCUS AND AGENDA | 93

- **M: Meaning** (What makes this important?)
- **M: Measurement** (How will you know when you have it?)
- **Y: Starting Point** (Where do YOU want to start?)

Some people feel that 'outcome' is a bit too goal focused and may not serve some clients, so we offer our amended acronym, TUMMY:

- **U: Useful** (What would be useful to you today?)

While these five elements are listed as a series of questions, this is not a script. The journey from opening a conversation to truly understanding what a client wants and needs is a process that should not be rushed, so there will be space between these elements. It is through partnership and targeted curiosity that the focus and agenda is revealed. The exercises we have chosen are meant to help the coaches relax and play with this sometimes elusive skill.

SUGGESTED WARMUPS

WARMUP 1: Agenda Reflection Circle

STRUCTURE
This exercise involves the whole group and engages the coaches in reflecting as a tool for helping set an agenda.

INSTRUCTIONS

- Create a circle.
- The first person in the circle is the client. The second person is the coach.
- The client takes up to one minute to explain their topic/focus without interruption by the coach.

- Based on what the client has shared, the coach reflects their understanding of the client's values, strengths and desires to help the client become clearer on what they want. If it has emerged, the coach might also reflect their understanding of what the client wants from the session.
- For this coach and client pair, this is the end of the conversation.
- The coach from that conversation then becomes the client for the next person in the circle.
- Continue until all participants have been in both roles.

Debrief

- What did you learn from this exercise?

WARMUP 2: BNA Group Coaching - Agenda

Structure

This exercise involves the whole group with one member of the group as the client and the rest of the group as coaches, that is, one client and many coaches. We sometimes call this BNA's version of group coaching, or reverse group coaching.

Instructions

- Choose one member of the group to be the client.
- Each participant will drag the client's Zoom box to the center of their screen so the client is surrounded by the coaches. If in person, the coaches can be in a semi-circle facing the client.
- The client takes up to one minute to explain their topic or focus without interruption by a coach.

- Based on what the client has shared, three different coaches reflect their understanding of the client's values, strengths and desires to help the client become clearer on what they want. If it has emerged, coaches might also reflect their understanding of what the client wants from the session.
- After three coaches have shared, the client responds however they would like in further clarifying their chosen focus. The client doesn't say who they're answering (it doesn't matter, and could be a combo). They can make any statement they wish to make.
- Based on the client statement, three more coaches offer reflections or questions to further refine.
- This continues until the group has come to a clear agenda for the session.

Debrief

- What did you learn from this exercise?

~

Coaching with a Twist: Focus and Agenda

Structure

In this *Coaching with a Twist*, the coach and client will engage until the coach-client agreement has been established. The coach-client agreement has been created when the coach and client clearly understand what the client wants to work on, what they would like to have by the end of the session and how they would like to use the time. When the coach believes there is a clear agenda, they should verify it with the client.

Instructions

- **Participants:** 1 coach, 1 client
- **Time frame:** The time frame is however long it takes to get to a clear agenda.
- **Client:** Choose an area of focus that is authentic (i.e., real play versus role play).
- **Coach:** Coach with the intention of creating the coach-client agreement. When the agreement is clear, the exercise ends. Keep the conversation real. Don't pretend you have a past or future with this client - unless you do.
- **Facilitator/Timekeeper:** If after five minutes, there's no agenda and it doesn't seem to be moving in that direction, remind the coach to establish the agenda.
- **Observers:** If on Zoom, turn off camera and audio during the coaching, and avoid writing in the chat as this can distract the coach and client.

Debrief

Elicit the coach's experience of focusing on setting a clear agenda.

- What did you learn from that?

Observers and client:

- What did you notice?
- What did the coach do that was skillful and effective?
- What moments stood out for you?

Closing the Session

After everyone has had a turn to serve as either coach or client, invite each person in the group to share what they are taking away from the session.

LESSON PLAN 6: INFORMATION SHARING

Many challenges come up around information sharing. Before we address some of those challenges, we want to note that the longer we've coached, the less we share information. Often coaches feel that if they don't offer resources or information, then their clients aren't getting enough value. But this is not true. Our job is facilitating client growth and learning. Sometimes, this may include helping a client source information.

We find that most people are not held back by a lack of information. What we notice in clients is often an issue of having **too much information.** There's so much out there on the internet that a person could easily be overwhelmed by, for example, 17 different diets all promising to be "the one." In cases like this, we see the coach's role as helping the client clarify what information they're seeking and to what ends (i.e., What are the real goals?) We might ask: "What is your criteria for sorting information?" "What sources do you trust and why?" Ideally, we're not just working with clients to solve a particular issue but also to develop their ability and methodology to solve future information needs.

Sometimes a continuing search for information may be masking ambivalence (e.g., "If only I found the exact right information, then I would…."). For the most part, people know what they should do differently and have the information they need to make it happen; they just haven't found the way of making the change that works for them. Bottom line: share minimally, and if and when you do, do it in a coach-consistent manner.

How Much Should We Share?

> **Betsy:** *When I started out, I gave clients a LOT of information — usually a few websites, a couple of book recommendations and maybe a podcast — figuring my clients would want to know everything, and they could pick and choose what works for them. This usually resulted in them using none of the resources.*

What works best is to narrow down exactly what the client wants or needs and then offer a specific resource or targeted bit of information which, with permission of the client, can be shared during or after the session.

What if I Don't Know the Answer?

That's fine. We often don't know the answer or have expertise in the client's field or area of interest. Our expertise is in coaching, not every topic that a client is looking to work on. In fact, there are many advantages to not knowing the answers, perhaps most importantly that our not knowing empowers clients to find their own answers. We should, however, be transparent about what we know and don't know.

If it's something you have some knowledge of, but not at the tip of your fingers, you might offer to check your resources after the session, or to send them referrals (e.g., nutritionist, therapist, lawyer). But you can also explore with them how they can go about finding the answers or experts they seek.

What Should We Share? What Are Trustworthy vs. Non-trustworthy Sources?

While sharing information skillfully is common to all types of coaches, the issue of reliable sources may be a bigger issue in health coaching versus other types of coaching for several reasons:

- Because health coaches are medical adjacent, clients may not be aware of scope of practice and may assume any resources shared are medically accurate. (The National Board of Health and Wellness Coaches (NBHWC) sets out parameters around evidence-based information.)
- These days, the area of health and wellness seems particularly prone to misinformation and disinformation in ways that can be harmful.

While these issues may not apply in business and leadership coaching, choosing evidence-based resources is highly recommended regardless of the type of coaching you do.

In this session, we typically brainstorm the question around trustworthy vs untrustworthy sources, starting with the untrustworthy sources (it's more fun!). Among the non-trusted sources are posts on social media that are the opinion of an influencer. Among trusted sources we would include those recommended by the NBHWC and various peer-reviewed studies. It's imperative that coaches know how to assess the reliability of information sources.[1]

For coaches who work with leaders and executives, clients may have an expectation for their coaches to share information, ideas, research and perspectives. Consider your client, the impact of sharing on the partnership and the coaching agreement you have with them.

What Do I Do if the Client Keeps Asking Me to Tell Them What to Do?

Sometimes a client does not want or need coaching but something else. So we can use our skills to better understand the client's needs while always being in service to the client.

Sometimes the client really does need specific information (e.g., nutritional recommendations), which may be out of scope for a coach. In this case, it's important to explore what the client wants, share what the coach can do to support the client, clarify scope of practice and if the need is out of scope, discuss how the client can find the right support or resource.

What is Out of Scope for Me to Share as a Coach?

Among the areas that are out of scope for a coach are meal plans, nutritional advice, recommending or suggesting supplements, diagnosing, treating, legal, financial, tax or other types of advice that require licensure. (Surgery is also out of scope — unless you're a surgical coach.)

How Can I Respond to Client Requests Most Effectively?

This is covered in one of the warm-up exercises below. First, acknowledge the client's request, need or desire; second, clarify what the client really wants to know. Third, coach from there. When sharing what you don't do (e.g., tell people what to do, give nutritional advice), also share why you don't do that (e.g., "It's out of my scope of practice," "I don't have expertise in that area," "Our current contract does not allow for consulting, but if you're interested in that, we can recontract.")

What is E-P-E or A-O-A?

These terms come from Motivational Interviewing and stand for Elicit-Provide-Elicit and Ask-Offer-Ask, respectively. Sometimes this is also called A-A-O-A or Ask, Ask, Offer, Ask.

The first E or A might be something like:

- "What specifically are you looking for?"
- "In what ways would this information help you?"
- "What do you already know about this?"

Then we would ask permission:

- "Would you be interested in a resource on that topic?"
- "May I share an idea with you?"

In the A-A-O-A case, the first two questions (or asks) cover what the client wants to know and permission for the coach to share.

Once the client has affirmed interest, you would share a digestible amount of information [the P(rovide) or O(ffer)]. This might be, for example: a technique, a handout, information on a certain kind of diet or a pattern that the coach has noticed over time.

The last E(licit) or A(sk) checks in with the client on what was shared, affirming the client's autonomy. An example might be, "What are your thoughts about that?" The coach might say earlier, "With your permission, I can offer a resource, and then I'd love to know if and how that resonates for you."

When Might it Be Important to Share if a Client Has Not Asked for Information?

If we have seen or sensed a red flag, it's important to raise it. (For more, see A Note on Red Flags in the Introduction to Part 3.)

Are We Only Talking about Sharing Information?

No, we're also talking about sharing observations, ideas, thoughts, stories, etc.

What if My Job has Predetermined Coaching Protocols?

One more area of challenge around information sharing can happen when a coach is employed at a health tech or other company and is given protocols to use with clients. For example, a coach may be given a predetermined focus or agenda (e.g., sleep hygiene). In this case, the coach might offer to the client, "I have a possible topic we can work on today, which I can share, but that does not limit you; ultimately you will decide what is most important to you in how we use our time today. How does that sound?"

SUGGESTED WARMUPS

For this particular lesson, we recommend discussing issues and challenges around information sharing before doing the warmups. This will ensure everyone has enough information about coaching behavior and non-coaching behavior. We like to elicit the group's knowledge before adding our own thoughts, ideas and information.

WARMUP 1: Out-of-Scope Request Circle with Inappropriate Coach Response

<u>Structure</u>
This exercise involves the whole group and highlights non-coach-consistent responses to out-of-scope requests.

Lesson Plan 6: INFORMATION SHARING | 103

INSTRUCTIONS

- Create a circle.
- Person One is the client and Person Two is the coach.
- The client will make a request to the coach that is broad or out of scope.
- The coach responds with a **non**-coach-consistent or out-of-scope response.
- This continues until everyone has been in both roles.

EXAMPLE

Client: Tell me which diet would be best for me.
Coach: Oh, I have this friend who just lost a lot of weight eating nothing but baru nuts. You should definitely do it.

WARMUP 2: Out-of-Scope Request Circle with Skilled Coach Response

STRUCTURE
This exercise involves the whole group and highlights coach-consistent responses to out-of-scope requests.

INSTRUCTIONS

- Create a circle.
- Person One is the client and Person Two is the coach.
- The client will make a request to the coach that is broad or out of scope.
- In responding to the client, the coach will follow five steps:
    1. Acknowledge the client's need/ask/request.
    2. Decline to provide it.
    3. Explain why.

4. Share what you can do to help address the client's needs.
5. Check in with the client.

- After the client has made the request and the coach has responded, the conversation ends.
- The coach then becomes the next client.
- Continue until everyone has done both roles.

Example

Client: Tell me which diet would be best for me.
Coach: I understand you're looking for a way of eating that would be best for you. I can't tell you that because recommending a particular diet is out of scope for a health coach. What we can do is explore more about what you want in a diet and determine what resources might be helpful. For needs outside of my scope, such as a nutritionist or other provider, we can also discuss how to access them. How does that sound?

Debrief

- What did you notice?
- What was useful about that exercise?

WARMUP 3: Group Exercise - Info Request Batting Practice

Structure

This involves the group in no particular order. The facilitator will offer a client statement and participants will offer responses. There can be many reflections for each client statement.

Instructions

- The facilitator offers one of the following client statements:
  - "I've decided I'm going to run a marathon. I've never run before but know it's important to train, so I'm going to start with 10 miles a day."
  - "What diet should I be eating?"
  - "I want to be a good leader. I know you have a lot of clients who are leaders. Can you tell me how?"
  - **Make up your own — or better yet, elicit from the group something a client has said that was really challenging. (This one is usually the best!)**
- Multiple participants offer responses, one at a time. There is no limit to how many different responses can be offered. Be creative. Take chances. Reflect or ask a question that helps to narrow down the need or request. Remember to elicit what the client already knows.
- Repeat with other client statements. We recommend at least three rounds.

Debrief

- What did you notice?
- What was useful about that exercise?

Coaching with a Twist: Information Sharing

In this *Coaching with a Twist*, the coach practices how to navigate when a client keeps asking the coach what to do.

Instructions

- **Participants:** 1 coach, 1 client
- **Time frame:** This usually takes about 5 - 7 minutes of coaching but is not time restricted as it ends whenever the coach has responded to the fifth request.
- **Client:** In this case, you will most likely role play. You can choose any topic, including a request that the coach could not possibly know the answer to or is out of scope. It can be something that is real for you or you can channel a real or imaginary challenging client. Continue to ask the coach to tell you what you should do five times. Don't worry about being a pain in the butt or a difficult client. It's kind of the point of this exercise.
- **Coach:** Play with five different ways to respond to the client without telling the client what to do. Each and every time the client asks, the coach must respond in a coach-consistent manner. Play with different ways of doing so. Use the framework of a coaching session, which includes establishing an agenda (the agreement between the client and coach regarding the client's focus and desired outcome). Keep the conversation real. Don't pretend you have a past or future with this client — unless you really do.
- **Facilitator/Timekeeper:** Count the number of times the client has requested information or direction, and end the conversations when the coach has responded the fifth time.
- **Observers:** If on Zoom, turn off camera and audio during

the coaching, and avoid writing in the chat as this can distract the coach and client.

Debrief

Elicit from both the coach and then the client their experience.

- What did you learn from that?
- What was useful?

Observers:

- What did you notice?
- What did the coach do that was skillful and effective?
- What moments stood out for you?

Closing the Session

After everyone has had a turn to serve as either coach or client, invite each person in the group to share what they are taking away from the session.

LESSON PLAN 7: STAGES OF CHANGE

Clients (and the rest of us) are often frustrated that they haven't already made the changes they want to, or they haven't made progress. This often results from a lack of understanding of the process of change.

The Transtheoretical Model (also called the Stages of Change Model, or TTM), developed by Prochaska and DiClemente,[1] states that people move through five stages of change:

1. **Precontemplation** (not ready for change)
2. **Contemplation** (thinking about change)
3. **Preparation** (preparing for action)
4. **Action** (taking action)
5. **Maintenance** (maintaining a positive behavior)

For each stage of change, different strategies, which the model lays out, are effective for helping a client move to the next stage. Clients may stay in a particular stage for many sessions or they may shift from stage to stage within a session.

BELOW ARE examples of strategies for each stage:

1. **Precontemplation:** Build awareness for the need to change
2. **Contemplation:** Increase pros for change and decrease cons
3. **Preparation:** Commit, develop resources, plan
4. **Action:** Implement and revise plan
5. **Maintenance:** Integrate change into lifestyle, handle setbacks

While the Transtheoretical Model is an important source for those working in behavior change, the Stages of Change model can be helpful with all kinds of coaching — and for understanding ourselves and other people in our life.

We've found it to be a useful tool when we notice resistance or challenges in coaching, which can often come from a mismatch in what stage of change the client is in versus which stage the coach thinks the client is in. For example, if the client says they want to run five miles a day, and the coach assumes they are ready to do it now but the client is really at the stage of researching footwear, the client may feel pressured or even commit to action steps that they're not ready for. If a client fails to meet their goals repeatedly, this can be discouraging and decrease self-efficacy. In the example above, the client is likely in the Preparation stage, but the coach is coaching as if the client is in Action.

It's important for coaches to be aware of any judgments they may hold about a client's stage of change. Often coaches think clients should be in Action but in reality, most coaching takes place at earlier stages, which is when coaching can have the biggest impact.

This lesson is designed to help recognize what stage a client is in and to coach accordingly. It's important to recognize that people can shift in either direction when moving between the stages. A person can move forward and a person can go backward along the stages of change.

While forward and backward would suggest judgment, we do not mean it that way. There are often very good reasons to move to earlier stages in the model, and it's normal to move in both directions. For example, a client may move into action but then stop because the action they've chosen doesn't really work for them in moving toward a desired goal. This presents an opportunity to go back (to Preparation) and develop a new strategy that might be more sustainable and enjoyable.

SUGGESTED WARMUPS

Depending on how familiar and skilled the group is with TTM and the Stages of Change model, it may be necessary to discuss the stages and relevant strategies before doing the warmups. During discussions, we like to elicit group knowledge first and add our own thoughts, ideas and information as needed.

WARMUP 1: Stage Says What?

<u>Structure</u>
This exercise involves the whole group and engages the coaches around what a client might say during each stage of change.

<u>Instructions</u>

- Create a circle.
- Ask for a coaching topic.
- Go around the circle five times, once for each stage of change (Precontemplation, Contemplation, Preparation, Action, Maintenance)
- For each stage of change, each person says something a client might say in that stage (based on the topic).
- <u>Note to Facilitator</u>: Write down at least some of the statements for use in Warmup 2.

WARMUP 2: Identify and Coach the Stage of Change

<u>Structure</u>

This exercise involves the whole group and engages the coaches around what a coach might say during each stage of change.

<u>Instructions</u>

- Facilitator will offer one of the client statements from Warmup 1 without saying which stage of change it was from.
- At least three participants in the group respond with statements or questions a coach might offer in response to the client's statement, based on what they believe is the stage of change.
- If a facilitator notices that someone has not participated, invite that person to offer something.

<u>Debrief</u>

- What did you notice?
- How might this be useful for you in your coaching?

Coaching with a Twist: Stages of Change

Structure
In this *Coaching with a Twist*, the coach listens for indications of what stage of change the client is in and coaches appropriately. There are no restrictions for the client.

Instructions

- **Participants:** 1 coach, 1 client
- **Time frame:** 5 - 7 minutes of coaching
- **Client:** Choose an area of focus that is authentic (i.e., real play versus role play).
- **Coach:** Listen for indications of what stage of change the client is in, and coach appropriately. Use the framework of a coaching session, which includes establishing an agenda (the agreement between the client and coach regarding the client's focus and desired outcome). Keep the conversation real. Don't pretend you have a past or future with this client — unless you really do.
- **Facilitator/Timekeeper:** Cue the coach after 5 - 6 minutes to bring the conversation to a close.
- **Observers:** If on Zoom, turn off camera and audio during the coaching, and avoid writing in the chat as this can distract the coach and client.

Debrief

Elicit from the coach and then the client:

- What stage of change did you believe the client was in?
- Are coach and client in agreement?

Coach:

- What did you learn from that?
- What was useful in focusing awareness on stages of change?

Observers and client:

- What did you notice?
- What did the coach do that was skillful and effective?
- What moments stood out for you?

Closing the Session

After everyone has had a turn to serve as either coach or client, invite each person in the group to share what they are taking away from the session.

LESSON PLAN 8: AMBIVALENCE

"All of us are ambivalent about something almost all the time."
– Ken Kraybill

Ambivalence is the state of having mixed feelings or contradictory ideas about something or someone. An indicator that clients feel ambivalent is when they are not sure, not committed or feel stuck. Signs include the client saying they really want to do something but then never doing it, or saying things like "yeah, but," or "I should." This stuckness may come from lack of confidence, ability, lack of resources, conflicting values or other priorities.

We've heard some coaches suggest that people who are ambivalent are not ready for coaching, but ambivalence is where the work of coaching may be most impactful. (See Lesson Plan 7: Stages of Change.)

It's not the coach's job to get the person to overcome ambivalence. Client autonomy is key. A client deciding not to make a change is a perfectly fine outcome. Our coaching task is to help the client resolve or at least understand the ambivalence and make choices.

One thing coaches may find helpful is to evoke the values and needs from the client that often underlie ambivalence and invite the client to name and explore them. Sometimes there are conflicting values connected to something, so you might ask how the client would prioritize these values or how they could honor both.

When reflecting ambivalence (see Lesson Plan 3: Reflections), name both sides using "and" not "but," ending with the desired change. For example, "I hear that eating with family and friends provides important social connection and that avoiding certain foods is important to improve your health."

Another helpful technique for working with ambivalence is exploring the client's vision. Once the client has an inspiring vision, you might ask, "What needs to be explored in order for you to move toward that vision?"

~

SUGGESTED WARMUPS

WARMUP 1: Ambivalent Language Brainstorm

STRUCTURE
This exercise involves the whole group and engages participants in exploring what a client might say when they're ambivalent about something.

INSTRUCTIONS

- Create a circle.
- The first person makes a statement that a person who is ambivalent might say. This could be something heard from a client.
- The next person does the same.
- Continue around the circle for several rounds.

DEBRIEF

- What did you notice about the energy in the room?

WARMUP 2: Story Using Ambivalence

STRUCTURE

In this exercise, the group tells a story together in which the main character is ambivalent. The story unfolds as each person takes a turn, adding a sentence to continue the story. We use the general structure of a fairy tale or children's story, starting with 'Once upon a time…' and ending with 'The moral of the story is….'

INSTRUCTIONS

- Create a circle.
- Ask the group for a theme for the story. The theme can be a combination of more than one suggestion.
- As the story unfolds, the main character will express and wrestle with ambivalence.
- The first person opens the story with 'Once upon a time…'
- Going around the circle, each person takes a turn adding to the story by contributing a sentence. Punctuation is implied verbally using inflection.
- When the story has gone on long enough, someone will say, "And the moral of the story is…" and bring the story to an end.

DEBRIEF

- What did you notice?

WARMUP 3: Ambivalence Circle

Lesson Plan 8: AMBIVALENCE

Structure

This exercise involves the whole group and engages the participants in shifting "sustain talk," associated with ambivalence, to "change talk." The coach helps the client make this shift by reflecting the client's values and desires. Sustain talk refers to statements that support maintaining the status quo, while change talk refers to statements that indicate a desire, ability, reason or need for change. Change talk signals readiness for change, whereas sustain talk reflects hesitation or resistance.

Instructions

- Create a circle.
- The first person in the circle is the client. The second person is the coach.
- The client takes up to a minute to speak about a topic that they're ambivalent about without interruption by the coach. Clients should choose something about which they have a lot of story. Make it real.
- Based on what the client shared, the coach reflects the client's values and desires (perhaps using "and" instead of "but" in a two-sided reflection).
- For this coach/client pair, this is the end of the conversation.
- The coach from that conversation then becomes the client for the next person in the circle.
- Continue until all participants have been in both roles.

Debrief

- What did you notice?

Coaching with a Twist: Ambivalence

Instructions

- **Participants:** 1 coach, 1 client
- **Time frame:** 5 - 7 minutes of coaching
- **Client:** Choose an authentic area of focus that you have ambivalence about (i.e., 'real play' versus 'role play.')
- **Coach:** Listen for ambivalence and help the client to explore, name and work through it. HINT: Listen for competing values, which often underlie ambivalence. For example, "I want to lose weight because I would feel healthier (value: health), but I want to be able to eat whatever I feel like (value: freedom)." Use the framework of a coaching session, which includes establishing an agenda (the agreement between the client and coach regarding the client's focus and desired outcome). Keep the conversation real. Don't pretend you have a past or future with this client — unless you really do.
- **Facilitator/Timekeeper:** Cue the coach after 5 - 6 minutes to bring it to a close.
- **Observers:** If on Zoom, turn off camera and audio during the coaching, and avoid writing in the chat as this can distract the coach and client.

Debrief
Elicit the coach's experience of coaching around ambivalence.

- What did you learn from that?
- What was useful?

Observers and client:

- What did you notice?
- What did the coach do that was skillful and effective?
- What moments stood out for you?

Closing the Session

After everyone has had a turn to serve as either coach or client, invite each person in the group to share what they are taking away from the session.

LESSON PLAN 9: EMOTIONS

"Language shows us that naming an experience doesn't give the experience more power, it gives us the power of understanding and meaning."
— Brene Brown, *Atlas of the Heart*

The *Improv for Coaches* session on emotion is designed to expand a coach's ability to help clients identify and name their emotions. By naming emotions, clients are empowered to normalize, explore and move forward from where they are to where they want to be. Expression of emotion is natural in the coach-client relationship. It's important for coaches to become comfortable holding space for the emotions of their clients and themselves.

Some people feel that strong emotions do not belong in coaching. We disagree. Strong emotions are an indication of what matters to a person and we take the positive psychology approach that emotions are information. There are no good or bad emotions, only those that are more comfortable or uncomfortable.

There may, however, be times when a client's handling of emotions may indicate a need that is outside of our scope of practice. Anne Betz shares in Lyssa deHart's Podcast, *The Coaching Studio*: "What I look for in terms of coaching versus therapy is the degree to which my client can return to us in observer capacity in their mind."[1] In other words, how well can a client witness their emotions versus being fully taken over by them? So the measure is not the depth of emotion, but rather the client's ability to stay present or to return to presence.

While coaches cannot diagnose or treat, we can talk about anything and through discussion, we can discover together if our client needs something outside of coaching. Often these other kinds of support will enable a person to return to coaching.

We've found it helpful during this lesson to offer some questions for discussion around emotions:

- What are situations you've had in your coaching where client emotions have been a challenge to you as a coach?
- How do you deal with your emotions as a coach?
- How do you recognize your emotion vs. your client's?
- How do you help someone in a distressed state to return to a more neutral state?

When eliciting emotional awareness in clients, note the difference between the questions, "How do you feel about_____?" which will more likely elicit thoughts and "What are you feeling?" which is more likely to elicit emotions and sensations.

This discussion could take place either before or after the warmups.

∼

SUGGESTED WARMUPS
These warmups are designed to increase the number of emotions a coach can identify and name.

WARMUP 1: Acting As If
We thank the improv world for this one.

Structure

This exercise involves the whole group and engages the coaches in embodying different emotions.

Instructions

- Participants start to walk around the space or, if remote, their own spaces.
- The facilitator calls out an emotion. A few examples are:

  - Fearful
  - Angry
  - Elated
  - Sad
  - Disgusted
  - Guilty
  - Surprised
  - In Love

- Participants continue to move about, taking on the emotion the facilitator called out; participants can include sounds, but no words.
- Give the emotion enough time (20 - 30 seconds) so that it's experienced fully and participants are challenged to access and explore that emotion for more than just a few seconds.
- After 20 - 30 seconds, the facilitator says, "Walk around in neutral."
- After about 8 - 10 seconds in neutral, the facilitator calls out another emotion and participants take on that emotion.
- Do this with at least six emotions, returning to neutral between each. We recommend ending with something on the joyful end of the spectrum.

Debrief

- What did you notice?
- Which emotion was the easiest for you to embody?
- Which was the most challenging emotion to embody?
- What does this have to do with coaching?

WARMUP 2: Emotion Brainstorm

Structure

This exercise involves the whole group and engages the coaches in naming emotions and emotional states.

Instructions

- Create a circle.
- Each person takes turns naming an emotion or emotional state until the group runs out of ideas.
- Allow for silence and thought so that the group stretches beyond the typical emotional states.

There are a great many emotions and there are no wrong answers here. We've even had participants make up emotions (e.g., chocolatey, narcoleptic, sizzling).

Debrief

- What did you notice?
- What does this have to do with coaching?

WARMUP 3: Emotional Mirror Circle

Structure
This exercise involves the whole group and engages the coaches in mirroring and naming emotions.

INSTRUCTIONS

- Create a circle.
- One participant, without saying what the emotion is, silently acts out or embodies an emotion.
- The next person in the circle mirrors the face and body and then guesses the emotion.
- The first person confirms or clarifies what the emotion was.
- Then the person who mirrored chooses an emotion and acts out that emotion for the next person to mirror.
- This continues until everyone has a turn demonstrating, mirroring and naming the emotion.

DEBRIEF

- What did you notice?
- What was easy or challenging for you in that?
- What does this have to do with coaching?

COACHING WITH A TWIST: **Emotions**

Structure
In this *Coaching with a Twist*, the coach is listening for the client's emotions. There are no restrictions for the client.

- **Participants:** 1 coach, 1 client

- **Time frame:** 5 - 7 minutes of coaching
- **Client:** Real Play — As the client, choose an authentic topic, preferably one that you have strong feelings about; this may include complex or confused feelings.
- **Coach:** Using the framework of a coaching session, including an agenda (the agreement between the client and coach regarding the client's focus and desired outcome), listen for emotions, helping the client name them and be with them. Keep the conversation real — don't pretend you have a past or future with this client — unless you do.
- **Facilitator/Timekeeper:** Cue the coach after 5 - 6 minutes to bring it to a close.
- **Observers:** If on Zoom, turn off camera and audio during the coaching, and avoid writing in the chat as this can distract the coach and client.

Debrief
Elicit from the coach:

- What did you learn from that?
- What was useful?

Observers and client:

- What did you notice?
- What did the coach do that was skillful and effective?
- What moments stood out for you?

Closing the Session
After everyone has had a turn to serve as either coach or client, invite each person in the group to share what they are taking away from the session.

LESSON PLAN 10: METAPHORS

"Metaphors are the paintbrush of the mind, allowing us to create vivid pictures with our words to explain our internal narrative or schema."
— Lyssa deHart

A metaphor is a figure of speech in which a word or phrase is applied to an object or action to which it is not literally applicable (literally in the literal sense, not in the way some people use literally metaphorically).

Clients often use language that is visual or could be turned into a metaphor, simile or analogy. As a coach, listening to your client's descriptions and language can offer you a window into the way your client feels or perceives the world. By exploring your client's metaphors and what they mean to them, you have an opportunity to help them deepen their understanding of their current beliefs and to create a new perspective that serves them if their current beliefs don't.

When we hear visual or metaphorical language, we must resist the urge to assume we know what our client means, and instead, ask them what they mean by the phrase or words they've used. What we think a client means might be quite different from what the client actually means.

Sometimes clients aren't necessarily clear on what they mean either, and the coach's curiosity can enable the client to clarify what is important and what they want. For example, if a client says they want to take a bite out of life, their coach might ask them what they mean by that. While unlikely, the client might say, "I'm a cannibal, and I really want to sink my teeth into my neighbor Bill." A more typical example might be, a client says they want more balance in their life and the coach asks what they mean by balance. This may result in the client stopping to think before giving a more nuanced answer.

We like to be inclusive, so for the purposes of this chapter, while technically not the same, we are using the word metaphor for both metaphor and simile.

SUGGESTED WARMUPS

WARMUP 1: Living Metaphors

Instructions

- Create a circle.
- Go around the circle with each participant sharing one metaphor that is alive for them right now (e.g., "I'm feeling sunny!" or "I'm slogging through mud")

WARMUP 2: Common Metaphor Brainstorm

Instructions

- Repeat the circle with each person sharing a common or cliche metaphor.
- Continue until the group runs out of cliche metaphors or you have gone around the circle three times.

WARMUP 3: Original Metaphor Brainstorm

- Going around the circle, each person makes up an original metaphor (e.g., I feel feathery. I'm a seahorse in freshwater).
- Go around the circle three times.

WARMUP 4: Story Using Metaphor

Structure

In this exercise, the group tells a story together using at least one metaphor. We use the general structure of a fairy tale or children's story, starting with 'Once upon a time...' and ending with 'The moral of the story is....'

Instructions

- Create a circle.
- Ask the group for a theme for the story, which can be a combination of more than one suggestion.
- As the story unfolds, a metaphor will emerge, and the storytellers will play with it.

Lesson Plan 10: METAPHORS | 129

- The first person opens the story with 'Once upon a time...' and completes the opening sentence.
- Continuing around the circle, each person takes a turn adding to the story by contributing a sentence.
- Punctuation is implied verbally using inflection.
- When the story has gone on long enough, someone will say, "And the moral of the story is..." and bring the story to an end.

DEBRIEF

- What did you notice?
- What does this have to do with coaching?

WARMUP 5: Metaphor Batting Practice
This exercise was adapted from the batting practice in Lesson Plan 3: Reflections.

STRUCTURE
This involves the whole group in no particular order.

INSTRUCTIONS

- The facilitator or someone in the group offers a metaphor that a client might use. For example:
  - I feel like I'm drinking from a firehose.
  - I can't get a grip.
  - I'm high as a kite.
  - I feel ungrounded.
  - I feel weighed down.
  - How do I land the plane?
- Multiple participants respond, one at a time, with a reflection or question for each metaphor. There is no limit

to how many different coach responses can be offered. Ideally there are at least three different responses per metaphor. Be creative. Take chances.
- Repeat with other metaphors. We recommend at least four.

Debrief

- What did you notice?
- What was useful about this exercise?
- What will you incorporate into your coaching?

Coaching with a Twist: Metaphors

Instructions

- **Participants:** 1 coach, 1 client
- **Time frame:** 5 - 7 minutes of coaching
- **Client:** Choose an area of focus that is authentic (i.e., real play versus role play).
- **Coach:** The coach listens for the client's metaphors and helps the client to explore them. The metaphor could be as simple as, "I'm jazzed." If there is more than one metaphor that arises in the session, feel free to play with some or all as it serves the client. Use the framework of a coaching session, which includes establishing an agenda (the agreement between the client and coach regarding the client's focus and desired outcome). Keep the conversation real. Don't pretend you have a past or future with this client — unless you do.
- **Facilitator/Timekeeper:** Cue the coach after 5 - 6 minutes to bring it to a close.

- **Observers:** If on Zoom, turn off camera and audio during the coaching, and avoid writing in the chat as this can distract the coach and client.

Debrief

Elicit from the coach:

- What did you learn from that?
- What was useful?

Observers and client:

- What did you notice?
- What did the coach do that was skillful and effective?
- What moments stood out for you?

Closing the Session

After everyone has had a turn to serve as either coach or client, invite each person in the group to share what they are taking away from the session.

LESSON PLAN 11: SOMATICS

As coaches, we learn to listen actively to what our clients say; yet, there is so much more information available to us if we learn to listen beyond words to the energy of the client and to our own energy and responses. By broadening our coaching presence and increasing our somatic awareness, we can increase the power of our coaching.

Using body-based techniques, we can learn to heighten our presence to signals from the client as well as our own body.

> **Amy:** *Some coaches have shared that at times they think they aren't good coaches. What I've learned from teaching movement is that our bodies communicate information. I encourage these coaches to check in and listen beneath their thoughts to what their bodies are offering. If something in the coaching conversation feels "off," it may not be anything they're doing wrong as a coach. It may be an indication of something going on with the client or a need to shift direction in the session.*

Through the exercises in this chapter, we explore how to tune into what our body, intuition and awareness are telling us.

SUGGESTED WARMUPS

WARMUP 1: Mirror Exercise
This exercise, which you can also find in the Glossary of Improv Games, is a gift from the improv theater world.

<u>Structure</u>
This exercise is completed in pairs, which requires breakout rooms for virtual delivery. Following the paired portion, the group comes back together for a full group version.

<u>Instructions</u>

- Each pair: choose the first leader and follower.
- Maintaining eye contact, face your partner like you're looking into a mirror. The leader moves their body, limbs and face. The follower mirrors the leader as if they were a mirror image.
- After about two minutes, switch roles so that the leader becomes the follower and the follower becomes the leader.
- After another couple of minutes, shift to having no leader. In this portion, each person follows the other. With no leader, things will tend to slow down as you each try to mirror exactly what you see in the other.

WHEN EVERYONE HAS RETURNED from breakouts to the larger "circle," do one more round with the full group in which there is no leader. Everyone should try to follow the others. The goal is to become so present and in sync that the whole group is doing exactly the same thing. It's very hard to achieve this, but a lot of fun to try. For those who do group coaching or facilitate groups, this is a great way to practice attuning to a group and everybody in it.

Debrief

- What did you notice?
- What did you notice about the connection with your partner?
- Did you have a preference for leading, following or no-lead?
- What does this have to do with coaching?

WARMUP 2: Somatic Check In

Structure

In this exercise, each member of the group contributes. This can be done verbally or by answering questions in the chat.

Instructions

- Let the group know if they should respond by chat or verbally.
- Ask the group the following questions:
  - What is the emotion you feel? Name 1 or 2.
  - What is a sensation in your body? Name 1 or 2.
  - What percentage present are you?

WARMUP 3: Somatic Reflection Circle

Structure

In this exercise, the person in the role of coach reflects to another person what they notice beyond words. (e.g., clothes, mood, environment, energy, etc.)

HERE ARE a few examples of this type of reflection:

- I notice that you're wearing bright colors.
- I see your business logo in your background.
- You look like you're exploding with joy.
- It looks cold where you are.
- You have a full bookshelf behind you.
- Your energy is warm and calm.

INSTRUCTIONS

- One person chooses another participant and shares a reflection about the person's energy, environment or mood.
- The recipient takes in the reflection, but does not respond verbally.
- The recipient chooses the next person and offers that person a reflection.
- This continues until everyone has both given and received a reflection.

DEBRIEF

- What did you notice about reflecting the person's energy, environment or mood?
- What was different from other reflections you have shared?
- What did you notice as the recipient of this kind of reflection?
- What does this have to do with coaching?

Coaching with a Twist: Energy & Somatics

Instructions

- **Participants:** 1 coach, 1 client
- **Time frame:** 5 - 7 minutes of coaching
- **Client:** Choose an area of focus that is authentic (i.e., real play versus role play). Don't worry about the somatic part — that's the coach's job.
- **Coach:** Intentionally reflect and ask about the client's energy, emotions, physical use of body, facial expression, etc. Pay particular attention to changes or shifts. (Many of us are unaware of what our bodies are doing when we're talking.) Use the framework of a coaching session, which includes establishing an agenda (the agreement between the client and coach regarding the client's focus and desired outcome). Keep the conversation real. Don't pretend you have a past or future with this client - unless you do.
- **Facilitator/Timekeeper:** Cue the coach after 5 - 6 minutes to bring it to a close.
- **Observers:** If on Zoom, turn off camera and audio during the coaching, and avoid writing in the chat as this can distract the coach and client.

Debrief

Elicit the coach's experience when energy and somatics were emphasized.

- What did you learn from that?
- What will you take back into your coaching?

Observers and client:

- What did you notice?
- What did the coach do that was skillful and effective?
- What moments stood out for you?

Closing the Session

After everyone has had a turn to serve as either coach or client, invite each person in the group to share what they are taking away from the session.

LESSON PLAN 12: NEW DIRECTIONS

"Oh, the places you'll go!"
— Dr. Seuss

In every moment, there are many directions we could go. Some choices may be more useful than others, but chances are there is more than one fruitful direction we could take. As coaches, we have habits or go-tos. The purpose of this lesson is to help access a greater range of options, to get beyond our first instinct or habitual response and to deepen our access to other possibilities.

We see this when we brainstorm with a client and ask, "What else?" The first couple of ideas are ones that are already floating around in our client's consciousness, but if we ask them to come up with three, four or more possibilities, then the client is likely getting into new, and sometimes surprising, creative territory. It doesn't mean their first instinct wasn't good. It often is. But ideally we want to give our clients space to consider options and then deliberately choose where to go. The same is true for us as coaches.

New Directions is, in essence, the idea behind all of *Improv for Coaches*, which is to become present and confident in the endless source of ideas that is accessible to us all.

Lesson Plan 12: NEW DIRECTIONS

One of the things students love best about *Improv for Coaches* is learning from the other coaches in the group. This is particularly true of this lesson, in which the coaches observe that there are different styles and directions we could go. Sometimes participants will notice that a particular direction at a specific juncture may be more powerful. Most importantly, seeing multiple possibilities builds confidence that there is no one right way to coach.

∽

SUGGESTED WARMUPS

WARMUP 1: You are so _____. I am so _____. (4x)
With gratitude to the improv world, particularly Mike Player[1] who introduced Betsy to this one. This exercise is a fan favorite of the participants in our groups.

STRUCTURE
This exercise involves the whole group.

INSTRUCTIONS

- The first player chooses another player and says, "You are so _____." The blank should be an adjective. It could be something like "smart" or "silly" or "compassionate." However, we encourage people to think broadly about these words and give someone something that might be a bit of a challenge, like "sparkly" or "magical," or "stinky" (or stony, purple, plant-like, effervescent...). The more the word is not something that the person normally identifies with, the more playful and creative they can be.
- Once you're given your: "You are so _____," you must respond four times with "I am so _____ ..." Try not to think too long about what you are saying and don't feel the need to be grounded in reality. The faster you rattle

them off, the more you will be accessing and accepting the sparks of ideas that are flying beneath the radar.
- The recipient then chooses the next person and offers a different, "You are so _____."
- Continue until everyone has been in both roles.

EXAMPLE:
"You are so ON FIRE!"
"I am so on fire we don't need heat in the winter."
"I am so on fire that I'm not allowed in national forests."
"I am so on fire people assume it's menopause."
"I am so on fire I'm bigger than Taylor Swift."

WARMUP 2: Group Coaching with a Twist

This warmup is a group version of this lesson's *Coaching with a Twist* and involves the whole group. One member of the group is the client and the rest of the group serves as coaches; that is, one client and many coaches. We call this BNA's version of group coaching or reverse group coaching. As always, we want to maintain the structure of the coaching conversation.

NOTE: Both the group and 2-person versions work best when the coach is succinct, using short, pithy statements. It will be helpful to have done three-word coaching from Lesson Plan 1 prior to this lesson.

INSTRUCTIONS

- Choose one member of the group to be the client.
- Participants drag the client's Zoom box to the center of their screen so the client is surrounded by the coaches. If in person, the coaches form a semi-circle facing the client.
- The coaching begins with any three coaches offering a statement or question to open the conversation. These will

be different because we are unique and use different language, styles and approaches. Ideally everyone participates at some point in the conversation. For example:
    - **First Coach:** Welcome. What would you like to explore today?
    - **Second Coach:** Hi (client name). I notice your joyful energy; what might you want to share.
    - **Third Coach:** Thank you for stepping into this conversation.

- After three coaches have offered something to the client, the client will choose a response (take your time). The client does not say who they're answering but makes the statement they wish to make based on the options they heard. That is, the client chooses the direction of the conversation.
- After the client has spoken, three more coaches offer a question or reflection to continue the conversation.
- Each time, the client chooses what to respond to and the conversation moves forward.
- After about five minutes or so, the facilitator will ask the coaches to bring the conversation to a close. That might sound something like this:
    - **First Coach:** What strengths do you bring to the experiment you designed?
    - **Second Coach:** I appreciate both the humor and the depth you brought to this session.
    - **Third Coach:** What have you learned about yourself from this conversation?

Debrief

- What did you notice?
- What did you learn?

142 | COACHING WITH A TWIST: IMPROV FOR COACHES

∽

COACHING WITH A TWIST: New Directions

The *Coaching with a Twist* in this lesson – which most participants find the most powerful lesson of the series – can also really challenge some coaches, as they must deal with repeated interruptions by the facilitator, work to stay present with their client, and go beyond their habitual responses.

STRUCTURE

The 2-person *Coaching with a Twist* is similar to the group version, except one coach gives all of the different options.

On Zoom, the facilitator uses two different visual cues: one to indicate to the coach when to offer a 'new direction,' and the other to indicate to the client when to respond.

You can use any two visual cues you'd like, but make sure they are neutral. For example, red and green might suggest green is good and red is not. Make them both fun and visual, ideally colorful and easily distinguishable. Betsy uses an orange cat finger puppet for "coach new direction," and a Siamese cat finger puppet for "client responds."

If you're doing this on Zoom, the coach, client and facilitator remain on screen. The facilitator will put the visual cue up to the camera to communicate a direction to the coach or client.

If in person, the facilitator can use verbal cues: "New direction" for the coach, and "Client response" for the client to respond.

The facilitator might cue the coach to offer three different options, but might also give two or four cues, or even just one. When the facilitator feels that the coach has gone in enough new directions, they will cue the client to respond. Until that point, the client must wait. The client may respond in whatever way they choose without saying what statement or question they're responding to.

IMPORTANT: The facilitator giving the indication to offer a "new direction" is NOT making a judgment about the quality of the statement or question offered. The facilitator is simply prompting the coach to look for other options in that moment.

INSTRUCTIONS

- **Participants:** 1 coach, 1 client
- **Time frame:** 5 - 7 minutes of coaching
- **Client:** Choose an area of focus that is authentic (i.e., real play versus role play).
- **Coach:** Respond to the visual cues as described above or audio cues if in person. Remember to be succinct. Use the framework of a coaching session, which includes establishing an agenda (the agreement between the client and coach regarding the client's focus and desired outcome). Keep the conversation real. Don't pretend you have a past or future with this client — unless you do.
- **Facilitator/Timekeeper:** Cue the coach after 5 - 6 minutes to bring it to a close.
- **Observers:** If on Zoom, turn off camera and audio during the coaching, and avoid writing in the chat as this can distract the coach and client.

Debrief

Elicit from the coach:

- What did you learn from that?
- What will you take into your coaching?

Observers and client:

- What did you notice?
- What did the coach do that was skillful and effective?
- What moments stood out for you?

Closing the Session

After everyone has had a turn to serve as either coach or client, invite each person in the group to share what they are taking away from the session.

GLOSSARY OF IMPROV GAMES

"Life is improvisation. All of those [improv] classes were like church to me. The training had seeped into me and changed who I am."
— Tina Fey

The games below are listed here because they were gifts from the improv community. (This is by no means an exhaustive list. There are a great many more exercises out there that are easily findable.) We are deeply grateful for the many improvisers, teachers, comedians and artists who have created, developed and shared these games.[1] If we knew who to credit each one to, we would, but alas we don't know who originated them. (We suppose we could improvise the attributions, but that might be closer to lying and someone's feelings could get hurt.)

The exercises in the Lesson Plans that you do NOT find in the list below are ones that we made up or adapted specifically for coaching purposes. We encourage you to make up some yourself.

You may recognize some or many of these games. They're frequently used in theater or improv classes and more recently, have been incorporated into workshops that focus on building leadership, communication skills and community.

In these descriptions, we share the "Zoom" version of the game. Any necessary adjustments for in-person versions will be provided following the remote instructions.

Some of the games are called different things by different people, so you may know the game by another name.

∼

A-Z

Person One begins a word or sentence with a letter (e.g., A, but can be any letter. Have the group choose the starting letter). The next person responds with a word or sentence starting with the next letter in the alphabet. And so on until all letters in the alphabet have been used.

The A to Z game can be used with one-word, story or any other format. It can even be used in a coaching conversation.

EXAMPLE with one word:

Apple
Branch
Catastrophe
Dangle
Epiphany
Fluffy

EXAMPLE using Story (starting with the letter "O"):

Once upon a time there was a chicken.
Pickles were the chicken's favorite food.
"Quick," said the chicken's friend, "I found a whole jar of pickles."
"Really?" said the chicken.
"Silly! Why would I make that up?"
"To mess with me; you're always teasing."

"Uh uh. not always."
"Very nearly always."
"Well, I thought you liked it."
"Xavier, what made you think that?"
"You usually laugh."
"Zippy told me I should laugh when something bothered me so it could bother me less."
"Actually, that's good advice."
"But not when you make someone think you like something you don't."
"Cool. I'll try not to tease you."
"Delightful!"
"Except on your birthday."
"Fuggettabout it."
"Geez, you're a tough customer."

∽

ACTING AS IF (aka EMOTIONS)

- Ask the participants to move around the space or if remote, their own space, taking on the emotion the instructor calls out; the actors use no words, but can include sounds. Here are a few examples of emotions we've used: - Fearful - Angry - Elated - Despairing - Sad - Disgusted - Guilty - Surprised - Nauseous - In Love
- Give each emotion enough time (20 - 30 seconds each) and then return to neutral (for about 10 seconds) so that each emotion is experienced fully and the participants are challenged to be in and explore that emotion for more than just a few seconds.

∽

CATCH

<u>Remote Version</u>:

- One person chooses someone in the group, says that peson's name and throws an imaginary ball to that person.
- The ball can be any shape, size or weight and the characteristics of the ball can change.
- The person who catches the ball chooses another person, says that person's name and throws the ball to them.
- Continue randomly until everyone's caught it a few times.
- This is a good one for a new group to learn each other's names and come together in the room.

<u>In-Person Version</u>:

You do not need to call out a name but instead face the person you are throwing to, make eye contact, then throw. The in-person version is more of a somatic experience and though the silent version won't build name recognition, it will build other awareness. There are, of course, many variations, and you can choose whatever you like. For example, you can have each person change the shape of the ball once that person receives it.

COUNTING

- In this exercise, the group counts from one to at least 10 and ideally far beyond.
- There's no order to who goes when.
- Anyone can say the next number (but a person should not say two numbers in a row).

- If two people speak at the same time, the group starts back to one.
- The facilitator starts by saying one.
- Keep going until the group gets to 10, but don't stop there. See how high you can go. We actually had a group (of eight) get to more than 100!

FIVE THINGS

Form a circle. The group is given a category (e.g., snacks, insects, rodents, vegetables, reflections) and the next five people name something that fits that category. For example:

CATEGORY: Insects:

1. Ant
2. Dung Beetle
3. Gnat
4. Fly
5. Grasshopper

CATEGORY: Reflections

1. Complex
2. Simple
3. Affirmation
4. Summary
5. Double-sided

The fifth person then chooses the next category. Do as many rounds as desired.

LAST LETTER

- Create a circle.
- The facilitator is last in the circle.
- The first person says any word they choose.
- The next person in the circle says a word that begins with the last letter of the first person's word.
- The next person says a word that begins with the last letter of the second person's word, etc.

We usually do three rounds of this game.

EXAMPLE:

- CharT
- TangO
- OctopuS
- ScatteR
- RanciD
- DastardlY
- YodeL

We almost always follow this exercise with Word Association (see below).

MADE UP YOGA POSES

(The coach version adds affirmations - see Lesson Plan 3.)

- One member of the group makes up an original yoga pose and names it. They can add "asana" to the name of the pose (e.g., pouring-coffee-asana). Anything goes here.

Silliness is encouraged. If on Zoom, you're still free to stand up and be more than just a head and shoulders.
- Share the name of the pose and demonstrate it for the group.
- Everyone in the group then does the pose.
- The person who made up the pose chooses the next group member to make up a pose.
- Continue until everyone has gone.

MIRROR

For the mirror exercise, break the group into pairs.

- Each pair: choose the first leader and follower.
- Keep your eyes open and face your partner like you're looking into a mirror maintaining eye contact throughout.
- The leader moves their face and body. The follower mirrors the leader. Movements can be subtle. Let your body determine where it wants to go. (2 minutes)
- Switch roles so that the leader becomes the follower and the follower becomes the leader. (2 minutes)
- In the third round, each follows the other. In this one, there should be no leader and things will tend to slow down as you each try to mirror exactly what you are seeing in the other. (1 minute)
- When everyone has returned from the breakout rooms or pairs and returned to the larger "circle," do a round where there is no leader and everyone tries to follow everyone else – to become so in-sync that everyone is doing exactly the same thing.
- Note: On Zoom, depending on the settings your "mirror" may appear to be flipped.

MOVEMENT & SOUND

- The first person makes a movement and a sound to accompany the movement.
- Everyone imitates the movement and sound.
- The person who made up the movement and sound chooses the next group member to go.
- Continue until everyone has had a turn to offer a movement and sound.

ONE-WORD EXPERT (aka THREE-HEADED EXPERT)

- Three players will be the expert.
- They will each give one word at a time creating sentences together, as if they were one person.
- Facilitator gets a suggestion for an unusual topic. Often there will be more than one suggestion and they can be combined into a novel area of expertise.
- Then anyone can ask the "expert" a question.
- The expert answers.

STORY

The group builds a story using any one of many variations, such as one word, two words, three words, questions only, one sentence each.

- Create a circle.
- The story begins with, "Once upon a time..." and ends with, "And the moral of the story is..." (Exception: omit this direction for the questions-only variation.)
- Each person takes a turn adding to the story. Depending on the variation, each person might add one word, two words, three words, etc.
- When the story has been developed, the facilitator or any one of the participants can bring it to a close by saying, "and the moral of the story is..."

WORD ASSOCIATION (aka FREE ASSOCIATION)

This is similar to the last letter game.

- Create a circle.
- The facilitator goes last in the circle.
- The first person says a word.
- The next person in the circle says the very first word that comes to mind.
- The next person says the first word that comes to mind, based on the word from the person immediately before.
- Continue around the circle.

We usually do three rounds.

EXAMPLE: Acorn, Tree, Family, Feud, Hatfields

WORLD'S WORST

For this game, elicit an occupation from the group.

- Anyone can step forward, or unmute in the Zoom version, and say or do what the World's Worst of that profession would say or do.
- Keep going until everyone who wants to has offered at least one impression.
- The facilitator can also decide when the first round is over, elicit another occupation and do another round.

Example: World's Worst PLUMBER

> "Oh, shit. Sorry about the downstairs."
> "I got no visible butt crack."
> "I hope you have a plunger and some other tools. I forgot mine."
> "Don't worry, I watched a bunch of YouTube videos."

Example: World's Worst VETERINARIAN

> "I hate dogs."
> "Achoo!!!! Sorry, I'm extremely allergic to cats."
> "Oh, I thought it was the left leg I was supposed to amputate."
> "Don't worry, I watched a bunch of YouTube videos."

In *Improv for Coaches*, we always choose the last occupation for the group:

World's Worst COACH

> We won't give any examples here because coaches will know exactly what to do and say.

YOU ARE SO _____. I AM SO _____. (4x)

- The first player chooses another player and says, "You are so _____." The blank is an adjective. It could be something like "smart" or "silly" or "compassionate." However, we encourage people to think broadly about these words and give someone something that might be a bit of a challenge, like "sparkly" or "magical," or "stinky" (or stony, purple, plant-like, effervescent…). The more the word is not something that the person normally identifies with, the more playful and creative they can be.
- Once you're given your: "You are so _____," you must respond four times with "I am so _____ …" Try not to think too long about what you are saying and don't feel the need to be grounded in reality.
- The recipient then chooses the next person and offers, "You are so _____."
- This continues until everyone has been in both roles.

EXAMPLE:
"You are so ON FIRE!"
"I am so on fire we don't need heat in the winter."
"I am so on fire that I'm not allowed in national forests."
"I am so on fire people assume it's menopause."
"I am so on fire I'm bigger than Taylor Swift."

IN THE WORDS OF PARTICIPANTS

"*Improv for Coaches* is a doubleheader. First, it's an absolutely delightful gathering of coaches filled with fun and laughter. Second, it provides a venue for tangible growth and intentional skill development. What a combination! Betsy and Amy have truly mastered the art of facilitating and cultivating a space in which you can learn AND play — I look forward to participating in more coaching improv in the future to keep my skills sharp and my heart a little lighter."

— Louise Buckley, NBC-HWC, ACC

"I was apprehensive about signing up for an improv class because I'm not an actress, but this isn't your typical improv class! After the first session, I was hooked. As a new coach, I struggled with being in my head during sessions with my clients. This class allowed the perfect environment to practice mindful listening, relaxing into coaching, and having fun with a group of coaching peers. 100% would recommend this class, and I plan on taking more!"

— Nicholle Chandler, PCC, NBC-HWC

"I highly recommend *Improv for Coaches* for anyone who wants a playful and powerful way to build their coaching skills. It's fun, and all the exercises make crystal clear how important it is to stay intuitive and fresh in our coaching sessions."

— Celia Alario, NBC-HWC, ICF Certified

"This was the most fun I've ever had in a coaching class. The skillful facilitation and format enabled learning and safety while trying new things."

— Jess Ahlum, MA, NBC-HWC

"On behalf of all of us at Motivational Interviewing in Medicine and Healthcare, I want to express our heartfelt gratitude for sharing your time, presence, generosity and expertise with us today. Your insights and exercises on the intersection of improv and coaching were not only informative but deeply impactful for everyone in attendance. Personally, I left with a greater appreciation for the power of being truly present, listening deeply and embracing the value of slowing down. Your willingness to be open and vulnerable during our time together is inspiring — a reminder of how essential this work is, especially in the world we navigate today. You two truly have a way of growing skills. You embody the coaching spirit and style to bring out the best in each of us, build upon what we already know and take us to new depths and heights in our coaching conversations."

— Jody Hereford, MS, BSN, RN, NBC-HWC

"This class has excellent content and is also a ton of fun! I came away with tools I will immediately put to use with clients. Betsy and Amy really know how to coach the best out of coaches!"

— Maggie Steig, PCC

"Amy and Betsy's *Improv for Coaches* program was one course I didn't want to finish because I enjoyed it so much! The way they hold space for a group of coaches to explore, play with and expand coaching skills was incredibly impactful. These sessions allowed me to stretch my skills as a coach, challenge some of my perceptions about coaching techniques and witness the undeniable power of *Coaching with a Twist*. I highly recommend *Improv for Coaches* to anyone wherever you are in your coaching career."

— Mary Anne Melear, CPCC, ACC

"I went into this course expecting it to be good and it exceeded my expectations. The content was innovative and it challenged me to become a more creative and joyful coach. Each session was engaging and focused on building new skills for seasoned coaches who are ready to learn something new."

— Leslie Spencer, PhD, NBC-HWC

"Thank you for a transformative learning event! Experiential learning is high on my list of priorities, and this class did not disappoint. *Improv for Coaches* is the perfect balance of learning while having fun — building coaching confidence and efficacy through purposeful play. I would do this again in a heartbeat."

— Wendy McLaughlin, MS, MCHES©, NBC-HWC

"*Improv for Coaching* marks a turning point in my coaching career. Coaching Psychology concepts like presence, reflections and questions turned from abstract into tangible skills that can be practiced, drilled and mastered through lighthearted play. One example of a game changer is mirroring. In coaching sessions, when I notice myself getting lost in a client's words, I now subtly drop into mirroring their body language and facial expressions, which grounds me and helps me better attune and attend to their message with grace. I can confidently say that all the games have impacted me in a similar way, profoundly shaping the way I communicate with everyone in my life and transforming my coaching for the positive."

— Iris Fernandez Valdes, NBHWC, CPHWC, PCC

"Improv changed my life and I didn't even see it coming. Improv has made me a better question asker, listener and investigator. It has given me creative and fun strategies and tools for interaction and developing rapport. I am more aware of body language and the external environment and am now completely comfortable with public speaking, whereas I wasn't in the past. Improv has helped me become a more aware, interesting and of course, witty person. If you're on the fence about taking your first improv class, let this be your sign: Do it!"

— Gerard Friedman, MS, ATC, NBC-HWC, Owner, Bell House Fitness

"It was an energizing and motivating experience. Succinct language can lead to such powerful, in-depth sessions. Less is more."

— Amanda Grubb, MA, MSW, NBC-HWC

"*Improv for Coaches* is an engaging, amusing and effective way to continue to grow as a coach. Betsy and Amy have designed a fun and safe environment where coaches at all levels can try new, creative approaches. I especially enjoyed the variety of imaginative coaching activities, the interactivity among the group of coaches, the hands-on practice, observation of others and immediate feedback. I guarantee you won't be bored. I would recommend this course to any coach who wants to be more assured and creative!"

— Carol Rosa Sabia, MCC, MBA, C-Suite Executive Coach

∼

"Improv in coaching? I'd never heard of it, but I got to attend a 2-hour workshop and was pleasantly surprised at how interactive and fun it was. What I really took away from this was how quickly we all settled and bonded."

— Parveen Johal, NBC-HWC, FMCHC

∼

"I highly encourage all coaches to take this class series! Rapport was built in our group right out of the gate and the environment that Betsy and Amy created provided such a safe and fun space to learn and grow. It was an enriching twelve weeks and definitely a worthwhile investment."

— Leonie Sztab, NBC-HWC

"The introduction of improv tools to my coaching practice has really helped me to loosen up and approach each coaching session with more flexibility and confidence. Loved this course!"

— Maggie Langrick, ICF-certified Wayfinder coach - Founding Publisher, Wonderwell Press

∼

"Betsy and Amy bring their wealth of expertise and their unique constellations of strengths to provide coaches an opportunity to play and learn in a safe setting. Whether you've been coaching a short time or for years, you will come away from their sessions with new insight, more confidence and a feeling of connection with other committed coaches."

— Joan Young, MA, NBC-HWC

∼

"Human interaction is complex. Coaching is more than listening and reflecting with your ears and mouth. This course helps to broaden your skills to encompass more of the complexity of human interaction through awareness beyond words. I take "regular" improv classes too. Improv has helped me tremendously both personally and professionally. Improv has been a game changer for me in all areas of my life!"

— Jen Uschold, PT, NBC-HWC, CPQC

"Your course has greatly influenced my life, coaching practice and how I teach others about coaching. I've referred many people to your course. I tell everyone the truth – that it is the BEST CE and professional development course I've ever taken!

I love how much coaching and improv have in common and for life in general. Listening deeply, saying "yes, and" instead of rebutting, allowing a space before responding based on what someone says, not what's been brewing in your head, are all effective communication and relationship building skills. I'm more comfortable with the process of "not knowing" what the client will say and trusting the coaching process as a result of this training. It allows me to shake off any annoying thoughts of having to be an expert and to trust in myself and the coaching process. I think the world would be kinder and happier if everyone had an improv approach in their communication and relationships.

I strongly believe in experiential learning and specifically learning through play. The skills I learned in your *Improv for Coaches* class have definitely helped me to be a better coach and to help other coaches to develop richer skills too. I've incorporated improv games into the coach training program I lead. Thank you for bringing more improv into the world! It is fun, playful, interesting, and skill-building, so valuable."

— Shelby Garay, M.Ed., NBC-HWC, FMCHC - Sr. Manager, Coaching, Headspace Training Institute

"This was the best course that I've ever taken (and definitely the most fun one). Looking forward to checking out your other courses!"

— Silja Sistok, NBC-HWC

"*Improv for Coaches* made me fall in love with coaching again! Betsy and Amy masterfully created a wonderful coaching container that allowed for joy, play, laughter and connection. I have become a more confident coach and facilitator because of this course."

— Vesna Antwan, PPCC, ACC

"Betsy and Amy have curated a course that teaches and hones skills necessary for good coaching. It's a fun and safe environment. You will feel challenged and cared for at the same time."

— Mikaela Davis, NBC-HWC

"Improv sounds intimidating for a person who tends to be quieter and more reserved. However, the instructor made everyone feel comfortable and relaxed so that it could be an enjoyable learning experience! I grew in my skills and never felt embarrassed. The group was small, which also helped."

— Jenny N., School Counselor

"You were both fabulous and held the space beautifully as you nudged us towards deepening our coaching skills. I also really appreciated that you both truly embodied fun and playfulness, along with masterful coaching tips."

— Shruti Sridhar Murthy, MBA, PCC, Leadership Coach

"Anna and I can't begin to thank you enough for the incredibly insightful training you provided for the Virta mentoring team. The warm-ups pumped energy and creativity into the team and the scenarios activity with affirming feedback proved to be a learning opportunity on so many fronts, as well as a chance to see what strong mentors we are. It really got our mentors out of their comfort zone and I think they were rewarded with a boost of self-confidence. Anna and I feel this sort of improv role play practice during our monthly meetings will be an excellent use of our time, to learn from each other and to improve upon our skills."

— Marlia Braun, PhD, RD, NBC-HWC - Senior Associate, Virta Health

"Betsy and Amy delivered an *Improv for Coaches* session to the Sayge Global Coach Community. They did a fantastic job in building a joyful team connection that inspired our coaches to bring new perspectives to their coaching and expand their skill set. Aside from an incredibly informative session, we had a few good laughs and were able to be playful throughout the session. All in all it was a fantastic way to expand our knowledge and connect as a community."

— Desiree Perez, MBA, MS, PCC

"Betsy and Amy are a great team to deliver this. Both bring complementary teachings and feedback. They make following the core competencies seem effortless (even though they're not!)."

— Sumom Geevarughese, MBA, ICF Professional Certified Coach (PCC), Founder, Steady Focus Coaching

"*Improv for Coaches* refined my skills, deepened my self-awareness and introduced creative strategies for becoming a more agile and adaptive coach. BNA Mentor Coaching consistently offers a supportive, enriching environment that fosters camaraderie and encourages plenty of humor."

— Amanda Nascimento, MS, CGC, NBC-HWC, Licensed Certified Genetic Counselor

∼

"Betsy and Amy are expert facilitators who create a safe and fun learning space for connection, creative exploration and professional growth. I feel much more confident in my ability to navigate a difficult conversation with lightness and ease as a result of taking the *Improv for Coaches* series!"

— Emily Hager, NBC-HWC, Detox Practitioner and Holistic Health Coach

∼

"The fusion of structured learning and practice with play is a refreshing reminder that growth can come from joy. The insights and mentorship to each of us during the sessions left me feeling inspired. Amy and Betsy's feedback delivery is warm, inviting and insightful. I can tell they have high levels of experience and applied knowledge."

— Lynn Marlette, NBC-HWC, A-CFHC

"The *Improv for Coaches* sessions were invaluable to me, not only in reinforcing key coaching competencies but also practicing various ways of responding to clients and using creative and fun ice breakers when needed. The course really kept me on my toes and stretched my intuitive coaching skills. Joining a talented group of coaches also helped demonstrate to me that there are many different and equally valid ways of responding to a client's needs."

— Kathy Osvath, Mayo Clinic Certified Wellness Coach, ACC, Retired Faculty, Federal Executive Institute

"*Improv for Coaches* is like a sip of micro-brew Kombucha on a hot summer day—refreshing, cultured and a little different with just the right amount of fizz. It was such a boost to my confidence and coaching presence that I came back for a second round! Hands down, the most delicious coaching CE investment I've made."

— Noémi A. Sullivan, NBC-HWC, ACC

"Another wonderful learning event. Thank you, especially, for giving me such a glorious client (aka Margaret). I felt — truly! — blessed to coach with her. Learning so so much. I feel like you're, with the help of this collective, helping me find my coaching essence again."

— Bev Lutz, MCC, MBA, CPCC Leadership Coach, Educator, & Founder at Center for Coaching in Organizations

"*Improv for Coaches* has once again helped me reconnect to my coaching roots. It's so enjoyable that I've taken the course twice! Even though I'm not coaching for my full-time work at this moment in time, I feel a sense of renewal and joy around my coaching skills, with more clarity about how I can apply them in my current professional setting."

— Louise Buckley, NBC-HWC, ACC

NOTES

Introduction

1. Barbara Fredrickson, "What good are positive emotions?" *Review of General Psychology, (1998):* 2:300-319.
2. Richard Boyatzis, Melvin Smith, and Ellen Van Oosten. *Helping People Change.* (Harvard Business Review Press, 2019).
3. Piaget, Jean. "Play, Dreams and Imitation in Childhood. Play." (Norton, 1962); Erica Chou, MD, Anne Graff LaDisa, PharmD, Amy Zelenski, PhD, and Sara Lauck, MD. "How to Use Improv to Help Interprofessional Students Respond to Status and Hierarchy in Clinical Practice." AMA J Ethics. 2023;25(5):E311-316. doi: 10.1001/amajethics.2023.311; Neel N, Maury JM, Heskett KM, Iglewicz A, Lander L. "The impact of a medical improv curriculum on wellbeing and professional development among pre-clinical medical students." Med Educ Online. 2021 Dec;26(1):1961565. Doi: 10.1080/10872981.2021.1961565. PMID: 34412576; PMCID: PMC8381956.
4. Edgar Dale. *Audio-Visual Methods in Teaching,* 3rd Edition. (Holt, Rinehart, and Winston, 1969).
5. Dufresne, Ronald L. "Using improvisation to develop leadership for a volatile world. Journal of Leadership Education." 2020 October. ISSN: 1552-9045; Schwartz BD, Rogers SL, Michels N, Van Winkle LJ. "Substantial Increases in Healthcare Students' State Empathy Scores Owing to Participation in a Single Improvisation Session." International Journal of Environmental Research and Public Health. 2024; 21(5):531.
6. Pier Vittorio Mannucci, Davide C. Orazi and Kristine de Valck. *Improvisation Takes Practice.* (Harvard Business Review. 2021.)
7. Stephen Nachmanovitch, *Free Play: Improvisation in Life and the Arts,* (Tarcher/Putnam, 1990).
8. Stephen Nachmanovitch, *The Art of Is: Improvising as a Way of Life,* (New World Library, 2019).

3. Rules of Improv

1. Tina Fey. *Bossypants.* (Little, Brown & Company, 2013)

8. How to Give Feedback

1. William R. Miller and Stephen Rollick. *Motivational Interviewing: Helping People Change and Grow,* 4th Edition. (The Guilford Press, 2023).
2. David L. Cooperrider and Diana Whitney. *Appreciative Inquiry: A Positive Revolution in Change,* 1st Edition. (Berrett-Koehler Publishers, 2005)

3. Nonviolent Communication (NVC), developed by Marshall Rosenberg, is a communication method focused on expressing needs and feelings honestly without judgment, while empathetically hearing others' needs and feelings. NVC aims to foster empathy, understanding, and connection, leading to improved communication and conflict resolution. The four key principles of NVC are: **Observations:** Presenting the facts without judgment. **Feelings:** Honestly expressing your emotions. **Needs:** Identifying and expressing the needs behind your emotions. **Requests:** Making clear, specific requests instead of demands. Marshall B. Rosenberg, *Nonviolent Communication: A Language of Life.* (Jalmar Press, 1998).

Introduction to Part 3

1. BNA Mentor Coaching: https://bnamentorcoaching.com (see Resources page).

Lesson Plan 1: SUCCINCTNESS

1. Throughout the book, in cases where we did not create an exercise, we acknowledge them as gifts from the improv theater world. We refer to these gifts this way because we do not know who originally created them. There are, however, many great creators and teachers of improv theater and it's possible that some of the exercises could be traced back to their work. A few classic books include:
    VIOLA SPOLIN. *Improvisation for the Theater: A Handbook of Teaching and Directing Techniques (Drama and Performa*nce *Studies)*, 3rd ed. (Northwestern University Press, 1999).
    KEITH JOHNSTONE. *Impro: Improvisation and the Theatre* (Methuen Drama, 2007).
    AUGUSTO BOAL. *Theater of the Oppressed.* (Theatre Communications Group, 1993).

Lesson Plan 2: QUESTIONS

1. Red Flags Guidebook and Red Flags Coaching Demo can be found here: https://bnamentorcoaching.com/free-resources

Lesson Plan 3: REFLECTIONS

1. Motivational Interviewing & Beyond. "Affirmation and Praise" (S01E03) *YouTube*, 22 September. 2020, https://www.youtube.com/watch?v=48331Fg2c6Q&t=3s
2. William R. Miller and Stephen Rollick. *Motivational Interviewing: Helping People Change and Grow,* 4th Edition. (The Guilford Press, 2023).
3. Motivational Interviewing Network of Trainers. https://motivationalinterviewing.org
4. Suzanne D. Alfandari, MS, LMFT. Shared in a professional development workshop for coaching staff at Ginger (now Headspace).

Lesson Plan 4: INTERRUPTING

1. Sustain talk includes statements where clients express reasons for staying the same, not wanting to change, or difficulty imagining making changes.

Lesson Plan 5: FOCUS AND AGENDA

1. The TOMMY model was shared at a webinar at the WBECS coaching summit by coaching.com (2023).

Lesson Plan 6: INFORMATION SHARING

1. Some resources include: https://www.stevenson.edu/online/about-us/news/how-to-identify-reliable-information/; https://library.georgetown.edu/tutorials/research-guides/evaluating-internet-content; https://researchguides.ben.edu/source-evaluation. Or better yet, research this on your own.

Lesson Plan 7: STAGES OF CHANGE

1. James O. Prochaska, John Norcross and Carlo DiClemente. *Changing for Good: A Revolutionary Six-Stage Program for Overcoming Bad Habits and Moving Your Life Positively Forward.* (Quill, 1994).

Lesson Plan 9: EMOTIONS

1. Lyssa deHart. *the Coaching Studio.* Season 1 | episode 10 with guest Ann Betz, PCC. (2021).

Lesson Plan 12: NEW DIRECTIONS

1. Mike Player is a comedian and improvisor, and founder and director of comedy groups *Shock of the Funny, The Gay Mafia* and *Angry Daddies.*

Glossary of Improv Games

1. Throughout the book, in cases where we did not create an exercise, we acknowledge them as gifts from the improv theater world. We refer to these gifts this way because we do not know who originally created them. There are, however, many great creators, teachers and practitioners of improv theater, and it's possible that some of the exercises could be traced back to their work. A few classic books include:
    VIOLA SPOLIN. *Improvisation for the Theater: A Handbook of Teaching and Directing Techniques (Drama and Performa*nce Studies), 3rd ed. (Northwestern University Press, 1999).

KEITH JOHNSTONE. *Impro: Improvisation and the Theatre* (Methuen Drama, 2007).

AUGUSTO BOAL. *Theater of the Oppressed.* (Theatre Communications Group, 1993).

Acknowledgments

1. Salamon, Gabor. PhD. (Hungary, 2025). *Az improvizáció eszköztárának és szemléletmódjának alkalmazása a coachingban. (Applying the toolset and mindset of improvisation in coaching.)* Corvinus University of Budapest.

ACKNOWLEDGMENTS

Improv is not a solo game. There are many people who contributed to this book and to the development of *Improv for Coaches*.

It starts with our students who said yes to our workshops, helping us hone the courses. They taught us so much about coaching and humanity and gave us many great laughs. We're grateful to the companies and organizations that brought us in to work with their members and teams, including NBHWC, the International Coach Federation and its many chapters, Wellcoaches, Sayge, Virta, Avidon, Huddle Group Coaching Festival, and the Center for Coaching in Organizations Summit. All of these opportunities helped us expand the applications of this work.

We're fortunate to have generous graduates who helped us bring *Improv for Coaches* to larger groups: Celia Alario, Marlia Braun, Louise Buckley, Nicholle Chandler, Dara Crawford, Elizabeth Erna, Erica Evans, Liz Goulding, Lori Lubash, Christina Miller and Jason Olensky. A huge thanks to our excellent Demo Group of coach improvisors: Greta Cowan, Iris Fernández Valdés, Amy Goldfarb and Carol Sabia, who shared their vulnerability, humor and time.

We're grateful for colleagues who see the power of improv in coach education and have partnered with us in advancing both: Robert Biswas-Diener, Sophia Casey, Erika Jackson, Dominique Mas, Margaret Moore and Carmela O'Flaherty; and Lyssa deHart and Chris Vasiliadis who shared not only their coaching expertise but their experience in moving from an idea to a published book. We're also grateful to Gabor Salamon for reaching out regarding our shared passion and his work on improvisation and coaching.[1]

We wouldn't be writing this book without Jody Hereford, who taught us about compassionate leadership and facilitation, gave us space to develop new things and continues to champion us and our work. The talented Kelly Gorder has been an integral part of BNA Mentor Coaching, helping us develop BNA — with humor and wisdom.

The ADAPT Health Coach Training Program gave us the opportunity to train, mentor, assess, and learn from nearly one thousand coaches. There were so many talented people on our team, including Jody, Dotty Foley, Tijen Genco, Shelly-Anne McKay, Kelli Saginak, and our BNA Associates, Wendy McLaughlin and Melissa Pylypchuk.

We are greatly indebted to our readers Amy Mercieca and Louise Buckley, whose early feedback provided crucial guidance in the shaping of the book; and our readers Betty Broder, Kelley Brower, Greta Cowan, Iris Fernández Valdés, Amy Goldfarb, Janet Harvey, Arne-Per Heureberg, Micky Hillman, Michael Johnson, Maggie Langrick, Arlene Rahn, Tracey Rogers and Mary Vidal who all made it better (and tempered Betsy's impulses to share edgy humor).

We are grateful to Linda Herskovic for her patience and skilled proofreading and to Laura Sweet for her generosity and style. We credit the beauty of this book to the creativity and expertise of our designers Danielle Huthart, Lina Warshawsky, Lucia Ledesma and Yael Pardess. And last but not least, this book would not be what it is without improvising it into existence with Cooper Trinity Press.

Although we do a LOT together, we both have some people to thank individually. We're certain we missed people. Forgive us and thank you.

Betsy also acknowledges:

My colleagues from the improv troupes GUILTY CHILDREN and TERRORIST BRIDESMAIDS - including Max Burbank, Philip Clarke, Greta Cowan, Deb Doetzer, Dorothy Dwyer, Helene Lantry, Mary McCarthy, Susan McGinnis, Phil Lebovits, Jim Napoli, Tom Shillue, Scott Stiffler; my improv training with IMPROV BOSTON; Richard Averbuch; the LIVING STAGE THEATRE COMPANY, and Randy McKnight who introduced me to improv in 7th grade; improv comedians I play with in LA, including Mike Player and Jennie McNulty. My days of improv comedy, including the hell gigs, are some of my greatest memories. There were so many times when you made me laugh so hard I could not get my lines out.

Greta Cowan, my teacher, mentor coach and friend for going on four decades. Generous, hilarious, masterful, you preceded me first in improv comedy and then in coaching. Thank you for taking the course, for reading the book, for improving my coaching - and for road-tripping with us to the IOC conference. And now Amy and Greta are friends, too.

Adam Felber, a master improviser and as great a guy as he seems, who I've had the privilege to know since we were young improvisers in Boston, and with whom I briefly shared a flat - during Hurricane Bob, which was the type of non-event we all wish for now.

My earliest comedy influences: Lucille Ball, Lily Tomlin, Gilda Radner, Carol Burnett and Tim Conway.

Clare Foster and Stacie Chaiken for their partnership in my writing development.

Jim Wilder and Jane Schwartz for supporting my personal and professional development in life-changing ways.

Kiahna Watkins for reminding me of the power of improv to open up worlds. Playing with you and others at Aviva, Beverly Hills High and King/Drew Magnet High School taught me how to listen and was a big part of why I became a coach. Your talent and heart are massive. I love you forever.

My brothers who made up plays and puppet shows with me when

we were children (despite always casting me as a witch). My extended family, biological and chosen who have shaped me into whatever this is (no blame! just gratitude).

Michael Johnson, who has loved and supported me wholeheartedly on nearly every project I have undertaken and continues to be my number one champion, mate and co-parent to Chicken, Miep and Baby (aka Potato).

And of course, my partner Amy Warshawsky who said YES and we're doing this! What a gift to be able to spend so much time with you and to create together.

Amy also acknowledges:

My clients and students who taught me to be present and in service to their hopes, challenges and dreams.

My many teachers of movement, somatics, martial arts, self-defense and expressive therapies — Thank you for sharing your mastery.

Julie Kosey, Tammy McLennan and Kristen Truman-Allen — for starting my Mondays with heart and soul.

Arne-Per Heurberg — for inviting me to the Thunderdome and for your gift of friendship.

Kristen Bentley — for your mentorship. You will always be my model for transformational coaching.

Jennifer Davis, Wendy Bright-Fallon, Elissa "Duckie" Giessman and Mary Vidal — for being valued colleagues and dear friends through this process.

My family in the US and across the globe — with the addition of each in-law and new little life, my heart grows that much bigger.

Carrie and Ben. We did good. Mommy would be proud.

David, Lina, Kaya and Shai — I would not be me without you.

To you, my friend and business partner, Betsy Salkind, Rule #4 — There are no mistakes, only happy accidents. I am at my best with you at my side.

AUTHOR BIOS

Betsy Salkind and Amy J. Warshawsky are the co-founders of BNA Mentor Coaching, delivering experiential learning through group and team workshops and training.

∽

BETSY SALKIND IS CERTIFIED by the International Coach Federation (PCC), the National Board for Health & Wellness Coaching, and the Mayo Clinic. She served as a faculty member, Associate Director, Lead Mentor Coach, and assessor for the ADAPT Health Coach Training Program. She also works in health tech and private practice.

Before stepping into the world of coaching, Betsy spent decades making audiences laugh as a professional stand-up comedian and television writer. Her comedy credits include appearances on *The Tonight Show with Jay Leno*, Showtime's *Fierce Funny Women*, and writing for *Roseanne* and *Saturday Night Special*. She was also a member of the improv troupes Guilty Children and Terrorist Bridesmaids.

Betsy holds a bachelor's degree from MIT and a master's in Organization Studies from the Sloan School of Management. She's taught health empowerment to high school students and improvisation at MIT, Emerson College, AMDA, in corporate settings and for fellow coaches. Betsy believes creativity, curiosity and humor are essential to great coaching and teaching, and always strives to bring them to the work she does.

~

AMY J. WARSHAWSKY is certified by the International Coach Federation (MCC), National Board of Health & Wellness Coaches, and the Co-Active Training Institute. She was a faculty member in the ADAPT Health Coach Training Program where she served as a mentor coach and assessor.

Before becoming a coach, Amy worked in major community event planning, marketing and public relations. She was an Adjunct Professor at Bloomfield College in New Jersey and led a coaching initiative for the ICF Foundation in the Hoboken Public School District. As a leader and mentor coach, she has worked in a variety of industries with individuals at all stages of their careers.

Amy holds a bachelor's degree from Cornell University and a master's in Journalism from Northwestern University. Trained in a number of movement modalities, including martial arts and self-defense and in expressive therapies from Lesley University, she is passionate about bringing somatic awareness to coaching.

~

www.ingramcontent.com/pod-product-compliance
Lightning Source LLC
Chambersburg PA
CBHW020542030426
42337CB00013B/943